Collaboration and the School Library Media Specialist

Carol A. Doll

The Scarecrow Press, Inc.
Lanham, Maryland • Toronto • Oxford
2005

SCARECROW PRESS, INC.

Published in the United States of America
by Scarecrow Press, Inc.
A wholly owned subsidiary of
The Rowman & Littlefield Publishing Group, Inc.
4501 Forbes Boulevard, Suite 200, Lanham, Maryland 20706
www.scarecrowpress.com

PO Box 317
Oxford
OX2 9RU, UK

British Library Cataloguing in Publication Information Available

Library of Congress Cataloging-in-Publication Data

Doll, Carol Ann, 1949–
  Collaboration and the school library media specialist / Carol A. Doll.
     p. cm.
  Includes bibliographical references and index.
  ISBN 0-8108-5117-2 (alk. paper)
  1. School libraries—United States. 2. Instructional materials centers—
United States. 3. Instructional materials personnel—United States. 4.
Information literacy—Study and teaching—United States. 5. School
librarian participation in curriculum planning—United States. I. Title.
  Z675.S3D597 2005
  027.8—dc22

                                              2004013934

Contents

Preface

In the fall of 1998, I accepted a position in the Library and Information Science Program at Wayne State University. One of the courses I was assigned to teach was "The Media Specialist as Teacher and Instructional Consultant." The majority of my students were employed as classroom teachers while they took classes to become school library media specialists. As advocated by the American Association of School Librarians, a professional school library media specialist (as portrayed in this book) should hold credentials both in education and in library and information science. In this way, the school library media specialist brings both teaching expertise and subject knowledge of library and information science (including information literacy) to the school community.

To be effective in the role of school library media specialist, as defined by the course title, I felt that my students needed to learn how to collaborate with classroom teachers. A literature search in library and information science using the key word "collaboration" revealed numerous articles and books. These articles tended to focus on success stories or were designed to encourage the professional school library media specialist to collaborate. There were only a few articles in library and information science where it was possible to discover information about research on or the theory of collaboration.

Based on a tip from an educational psychologist, I discovered a rich body of work on collaboration in the educational psychology literature. In the intervening years, I have also found additional information on collaboration in both the broader literature of education and in the business literature. Using this information, I have been able to give my students the theoretical groundwork needed for them to become effective collaborators.

This book is based on my experience in locating, reading, and sharing the information about research on and the theory of collaboration, primarily outside of the library and information science field, with a few references from my own field. The intent of this book is to share with school library media specialists knowledge gained in other professions about collaboration that could help them initiate and develop collaboration in a public school setting. These techniques are appropriate for other collaborative efforts, such as the development of strong relationships between school library media specialists and public librarians in the same community. It is my hope that this work inspires more study of collaboration in library and information science, and also enrich current library and information science education.

Acknowledgments

Thanks to Mary L. Peterson, former student, for the indexing, and to her professor, Dr. Hermina G. B. Anghelescu.

Introduction

In the beginning, there were classroom collections or school library services offered through the public library. For example, prior to 1920, among the professional children's librarians employed by the Seattle Public Library, one was designated to work with and provide materials to teachers in the local schools. There has been continuous recognition among school library professionals that school libraries need the support of administrators, teachers, students, and parents if they are to deliver high-quality services. Also, throughout much of the history of school library media centers, working directly with students to create competent library users and to encourage recreational reading is consistently identified as an appropriate role for the school library media specialist.

However, the instructional role of the school librarian, as depicted in the body of national standards, has evolved over time. In terms of working with classroom teachers, the emphasis has been on building a collection to support the school curriculum and helping the teachers use appropriate materials in teaching. Sometimes library skills instruction is mentioned, but more as one element of the role of the school library media center than as an aspect of active curricular and instructional planning with teachers. So, today's vision of the role of the school library media specialist is not totally new, just expanded from earlier understandings.

1945 STANDARDS

In 1945, a subgroup of the Committees on Post-War Planning of the American Library Association wrote and published *School Libraries for Today and Tomorrow*. The standards identified these activities as appropriate for school librarians:

- Participation in curriculum studies and development
- Membership on teacher committees, both local and state
- Preparation of bibliographies for all reading levels and subject interests
- Planned instruction in the use of materials
- Cooperative guidance in development of good study habits
- Assistance in remedial programs, especially those related to study and reading skills
- Stimulation and assistance in group and individual investigation[1]

In many ways, today's school library media specialists continue to participate in these kinds of activities, which are still important in today's schools.

1960 STANDARDS

In 1960, the standards were revised and updated. This vision of quality school libraries lists these services as appropriate for the school librarian to provide classroom teachers in the spirit of cooperation:

- Collection development to support the curriculum
- Collection of professional materials for teacher use
- Acquisition of materials requested by teachers
- Guidance for teachers in how to teach library skills
- Notification of new materials
- Helping teachers prepare bibliographies on selected topics
- Providing information and materials as needed
- Serving as a resource consultant to teachers
- Delivering in-service training about library materials[2]

Other areas in the standards continued to stress the need for the school librarian to be involved in curriculum development. However, the recommended interaction with teachers stressed the delivery of materials more than today's more active role of instructional partner.

1969 STANDARDS

By 1969, the new version of national standards for school libraries had become a deliberate effort to merge audiovisual and school library services. They introduced the term *school media program* and gave the first indication that media specialists may take a more active role in the school:

> [Teachers] look to the media specialist . . . to keep them informed about recent developments in their subject areas and in educational trends; to channel information to them regarding students' progress and problems; . . . to instruct students in the use and resources of the media center as the needs of the curriculum indicate; and, increasingly, to assist in the analysis of instructional needs and the design of learning activities.[3]

These standards articulate an active role for the media specialist in lesson planning. While this element is only briefly stated, it is noteworthy evidence that the idea of cooperative or collaborative planning is not an entirely new one.

1975 STANDARDS

In the 1975 version of national standards for media centers, *Media Programs: District and School,* the emphasis was on districtwide media services. The index has only four entries under "teachers":

- Informing about media program
- Involving in school media program
- Professional resources for
- Staff development programs for.[4]

In the introduction, human interaction is identified as basic to the media program. "This concept of program focuses on human behaviors and interactions, with staff members supporting students and teachers and all other users in utilization of media to achieve learning goals."[5] Discussion focuses on the entire spectrum of media services available throughout the district and region; working with teachers is not addressed as much as in earlier versions.

1988 STANDARDS

In response to significant societal changes that occurred during the 1970s and 1980s, the American Association of School Librarians and the Association for Educational Computing and Technology again collaborated and produced the 1988 version of national standards, *Information Power: Guidelines for School Library Media Programs*. For the first time, the standards described and articulated the need for a different kind of working relationship between teachers and media specialists, which is: "a partnership among the library media specialist, district-level personnel, administrators, teachers, and parents."[6] Further elaboration states that the library media specialist should assist teachers with:

- Developing unit objectives
- Analyzing learners
- Evaluating current learning activities
- Developing the lesson plan
- Identifying appropriate resources
- Identifying potential logistical problems
- Securing needed resources
- Assisting in delivery of the lessons and unit
- Developing assessments
- Evaluating and modifying the lessons and units.

This vision for more involvement between the library media specialist and others in the educational community is explored throughout the standards; however, large portions of the standards still deal with the more traditional roles of working with students, collection development, and provision of materials.

1998 STANDARDS

In 1998, the American Association of School Librarians and the Association for Educational Computing and Technology published *Information Power: Building Partnerships for Learning*. For the first time, the term "information literacy" is used, and is defined as "the ability to find and use information—[and] is the keystone of lifelong learning."[7]

These newest national standards for school library media centers articulate and advocate for a role for the school library media specialist
working in collaboration with teachers to integrate information literacy
standards into the school curriculum. That is, the school library media
specialist must actively reach out from the media center and work to
become a full partner in the planning, implementation, and evaluation
of the curriculum, including the assessment of individual students. For
this to happen, school library media specialists must gain and retain the
support of administrators, and they must understand how to develop
and nurture productive relationships with teachers. This expansion of
the role of the school library media specialist can be difficult to sell to
other educational professionals.

To operationalize this new vision, it is now part of the school library
media specialist's job to reach outside of the school library media center and promote information literacy throughout the school. While
many education professionals are concerned about enabling students to
become competent users of information, school library media specialists have unique skills in the searching for, locating, and evaluating information. However, this expertise is often misunderstood by people
outside of the library and information science profession. Therefore,
school library media specialists must be proactive in planning and implementing curriculum in the school. In order to do this, they must establish positive relationships with administrators, who should publicly
support this role; work effectively with teachers; ensure that students
become information-literate; and educate parents and the general public about the value of this role. If the school library media specialist is
unwilling to become actively involved in programs throughout the
school, it is unlikely that administrators and teachers will ask for increased involvement of the school library media specialist. This lack of
interest is not caused by antagonism but usually results from the lack
of understanding of the role a school library media specialist can assume in the school. For example, the literature reviewed for this project rarely mentions the school library media specialist as one of the education professionals involved in school collaborations.

The danger in refusing to operationalize this new vision is that some
other group of professionals will come forward to ensure that students
become information-literate—because the need to teach information

literacy to students is both real and immediate. While the more traditional role for school librarians of using expertise in the selection, evaluation, and use of materials to support the curriculum may be more
comfortable, it is neither as challenging nor as important as the role articulated in the 1998 national standards. Clearly, information literacy is
within the professional expertise of school library media specialists. It
is time to implement the vision of the newest standards.

CONCLUSION

In today's world, the ability to use information effectively is becoming
increasingly important; in addition, the amount of information is ex-
panding exponentially. Students *must* become information-literate. At
the same time, taxpayers are more and more insistent that schools be
held accountable for teaching students. Professional school library media specialists already possess both subject expertise in the area of information literacy and teaching credentials. Now they need to integrate
those skills and bodies of knowledge throughout the curriculum.

Collaboration is key when working to implement the new vision for
the role of the school library media specialist in the school. That is the
purpose of this book—to give today's school library media specialists
an understanding of the theories that can help develop productive interpersonal working partnerships with administrators and teachers. It
also suggests specific techniques to use in the school setting to help
achieve successful collaboration and integration of information literacy
skills throughout the curriculum.

NOTES

1. American Library Association (The Committees on Post-War Planning
of the American Library Association, Division of Libraries for Children and
Young People and Its Section, The American Association of School Librarians), *School Libraries for Today and Tomorrow: Functions and Standards*
(Chicago: American Library Association, 1945), 14.

2. American Association of School Librarians, in cooperation with the
American Association of Colleges for Teacher Education, *Standards for
School Library Programs* (Chicago: American Library Association, 1960), 66.

3. American Association of School Librarians and the Department of Audiovisual Instruction of the National Education Association, *Standards for School Media Programs* (Chicago: American Library Association, 1969), 4.

4. American Association of School Librarians and Association for Educational Communications and Technology, *Media Programs: District and School* (Chicago: American Librarian Association, 1975), 127.

5. American Association of School Librarians and Association for Educational Communications and Technology, *Media Programs: District and School*, 5.

6. American Association of School Librarians and Association for Educational Communications and Technology, *Information Power: Guidelines for School Library Media Programs* (Chicago: American Library Association, 1988), 2.

7. American Association of School Librarians and Association for Educational Communications and Technology, *Information Power: Building Partnerships for Learning* (Chicago: American Library Association, 1998), 1.

CHAPTER 1

Collaboration: What and Why

In discussing the role of the school library media specialist in today's schools, it is important for everybody to understand the basic concepts underlying the ideas and theories involved. Often the other professional members of the school community are not antagonistic; they just do not understand who the school library media specialist is and what he or she can do. In Canada, the term used is *teacher-librarian*, and in many ways that terminology does a better job of communicating the full essence of this job in today's world.

The term *collaboration* is widely used in numerous fields and popular literature. For this book, *collaboration* has a very precise meaning. To start this discussion, let us define and discuss some terms as they are used in this book.

DEFINITIONS

School Library Media Specialist

The person in the school identified in this book as a school library media specialist has degrees both in education and in library and information science (or a dual master with coursework in both areas). At this time, some states (including Michigan, New York, and South Carolina) require both teaching and library science coursework for secondary school library media specialists. *Information Power: Building Partnerships for Learning* (American Association of School Librarians and Association for Educational Communications and Technology,

1998) stipulates that staff for a school library media center should include "at least one full-time library media specialist who holds a master's degree in librarianship from a program accredited by the American Library Association or a master's degree with a specialty in school library media from an educational unit accredited by the National Council for the Accreditation of Teacher Education."[1] Further discussion notes that the school library media specialist is "both a professional educator and an administrator on the school staff."[2]

This dual role acknowledges that the school library media specialist should be involved in educating students—and sometimes teachers, too. Keith Curry Lance has been involved in researching the effect of school library media centers on student achievement for years. Based on his research, he identifies the following activities where school library media specialists should be involved:

- Identifying useful materials and information for teachers
- Planning instruction cooperatively with teachers
- Providing in-service training to teachers
- Teaching students both with classroom teachers and independently.[3]

Information Literacy

According to the American Association of School Librarians (AASL), "Information literacy—the ability to find and use information—is the keystone to lifelong learning. Creating a foundation for lifelong learning is at the heart of the school library media program."[4] This is a broader view of what is involved in information literacy than that held by some other groups. However, this broader vision as expressed by AASL serves well as a goal for school library media specialists to strive to attain.

Information literacy, as presented in this book, means the student learns how to identify a need for particular information (personal, recreational, or curricular); knows how to locate, evaluate, and use information that satisfies that need; and is then able to evaluate the entire process just followed. While this could seem straightforward, the process is actually quite complicated. During the process, information located may necessitate rethinking and redesign of the original question; each step requires critical thinking to determine quality of any results and how to proceed from there, which indicates there is, or should be, continual evaluation of the process and its results. Overall, information seeking is a messy, evolutionary process. By developing competencies in this area, however, the student builds a framework that can be used for effective lifelong learning.

In 1998, AASL published new national standards for school library media centers, *Information Power: Building Partnerships for Learning*, which includes the definition of information literacy quoted above. These standards build a conceptual foundation for the role of an active, involved, collaborating school library media specialist and also explain and advocate that role in schools. An important part of that role is teaching information literacy and integrating it throughout the school curriculum. This is in direct contrast to the earlier, more traditional emphasis on teaching library skills. Library skills are more limited in scope, and information literacy reaches out from the school library media center into the whole school and all aspects of a student's life. Carol C. Kuhlthau is one of the leading researchers on teaching information literacy to high school students. She has skillfully articulated the difference between traditional and newer processes students need to learn. "Library skills prepare students to locate materials in a library. Information skills prepare students to learn in an information-rich environment. The concept of information literacy encompasses lifelong learning and the application of information skills to every day living."[5]

Collaboration

Webster's New World Dictionary defines *collaboration* as "the act of working together."[6] While this does communicate the basic idea, in the working environments of today's schools, the definition needs to be more fully developed to convey the magnitude of the relationship between teachers and school library media specialists advocated in this book. Marshall Welch, while addressing issues in inclusive education, says, "Collaboration is a dynamic process designed to achieve a shared goal."[7] This second definition comes closer to describing the extent of the ideal process that occurs between teachers and school library media specialists.

Collaboration, in the fullest sense of the term in this book, means that the school library media specialist and teachers in the school will work together to plan for, design, teach, and evaluate instructional events for students. This involves a long-term commitment and time spent together to develop both instruction and a collaborative relationship among the professionals involved. This type of working relationship between teachers and school library media specialists is truly a revolutionary change from the more traditional role of school librarian as a source of support for the curriculum.

This idea of collaboration builds on and extends two familiar roles—coordination of classroom and school library media center activities and cooperation between teachers and the school library media specialist undertaken to ensure coordination of activities. Collaboration is not cooperation; it is more than that. Collaboration is a partnership, and each individual brings important elements to the table. Teachers bring their knowledge of students in the classroom, expertise in their subject areas, and background in education and instructional design. The school library media specialist brings knowledge of the students in the media center setting (perhaps over a number of years), expertise in information literacy, and background in education and instructional design. Also, if fully involved in the school, the school library media specialist knows the curriculum and what is taught at each grade level. Everyone has something to contribute, and the students benefit.

Linda Corey notes:

> Through collaboration, [school library media specialists] and teachers work as a team to design learning experiences that are meaningful and developmentally appropriate. Together they can select the needed resources and develop the assignments that determine what the students know, learn, and understand. When [school library media specialists] are knowledgeable of content area standards, they are able to integrate information literacy standards in collaboration with teachers.[8]

This vision for collaboration between school library media specialists and teachers is vital in today's schools as all professionals work to educate students for success in today's world.

COLLABORATION IS WORKING TOGETHER

It must be stressed that the intent of this new vision is not that the school library media specialist "take over" responsibilities appropriately assigned to the classroom teacher. Instead, the school library media specialist would assume full responsibility for moving library skills and information literacy instruction away from isolation in the school library media center and into a state of integration throughout the school curriculum (as articulated and advocated by the American Association of School Librarians in *Information Power: Building Partnerships for Learning*). At the same time, the teacher retains—and even strengthens—the traditional role of teaching subject areas.

It could be argued that all school professionals are responsible for teaching information literacy. This is true in the same way that all school professionals are responsible for teaching reading and writing skills. This does not mean there is no need for reading and English teachers; instead, it reflects general acceptance of the importance of these areas. The same could be said of information literacy: It is so important that everyone must be involved, but there is still need for the additional expertise the school library media specialist can bring to this area.

The school library media specialist and teachers can address the entire range of instructional design elements. Jean Donham has identified a list of instructional design elements that successful collaboration teams work on together:

- Identifying student needs in accessing, evaluating, interpreting, and applying information
- Planning how and where the skills will be taught
- Relating this skill to other classroom learning
- Teaching in partnership
- Assessing the process of student learning
- Assessing the products of student learning
- Reflecting on the collaborative process.[9]

This means ensuring that the necessary information literacy skills are part of both the district- and the building-level curriculum, and that the media specialist uses instructional design skills effectively to integrate information literacy skills *as appropriate* into individual lessons and instructional units. In this way, students can learn to use information in the same way they learn reading, writing, and arithmetic.

As information literacy moves away from isolation, the school library media specialist retains responsibility for both teaching and evaluating the information literacy skills. At the same time, the appropriate information literacy skills for each unit are identified by a team made up of the school library media specialist and teacher(s). For example, the science teacher and the school library media specialist may be collaborating on a unit on seismology. Working together as full partners, they jointly determine what the unit will cover; consider the strengths, weaknesses, and current knowledge of the students; and discuss possible resources and teaching strategies. The teacher, of course, would teach and evaluate student learning for the geology and geophysical content for the unit on earthquakes. The school library media specialist would be responsible for teaching and assessing the students' ability to locate, evaluate, and use information in a variety of formats, such as encyclopedias or websites about seismology—the same as if the encyclopedia skills and website evaluation were being taught in isolation in the media center. At the conclusion of the unit, the teacher and school library media specialist would work together to evaluate the entire experience, examining the professional collaboration, resources, pedagogy, student experiences, and all other pertinent elements in order to determine what worked well and what should be changed next time.

It is vital for professional school library media specialists to realize, and to communicate to others in the school, that their professional training includes both teaching and the area of information literacy. Their skills in these areas can and should be fully utilized at both elementary and secondary levels. School library media specialists have an important contribution to make in teaching students to be information-literate. This is the goal of much of American education today, and the school library media specialist has a central role to play in this endeavor. In order to accomplish this goal, the school library media specialist must reach out from the media center and work both to create a climate where collaboration can occur and actively seek collaboration with teachers in the school.

LEVELS OF SERVICE LEADING TO COLLABORATION

There are many cooperative activities that occur in schools, but only one truly deserves the label of "collaboration" as discussed in this book. There is also a wide range in the amount of interaction or level of involvement that individual school library media specialists have with teachers in their schools. Several categories are presented below to help clarify the meaning of full collaboration, as advocated here.

Isolation

In some situations, the school library media specialist stays in the school library media center, welcomes people who come through the door, and concentrates on creating a well-run, well-stocked school library media center. Students may come to the school library media center on a regular basis for classes or literature appreciation, or teachers may bring classes to the school library media center, either as classroom lessons dictate or on a regular schedule. Also, students may come individually as they see the need for class assignments or for leisure reading. In this type of isolated, self-contained media center, the school library media specialist knows little about what is happening in classrooms. One possible source of information is the questions asked by students as they seek materials or answers in the school library media center. Another source could be comments made in faculty meetings by teachers or administrators. Overall, this low level of involvement with the greater school curriculum results in a school library media center that is dangerously isolated and may be vulnerable to cost-cutting measures because of the small perceived value it adds to the school community.

Cooperation

In the next level of involvement, the school library media specialist reaches out to the greater school community through bibliographies, announcements, and even casual conversations with teachers in the teachers' lounge and in hallways. There may be some attempt to identify current units being studied so the school library media specialist can provide materials appropriate for the lesson. If regular classes are scheduled in the media center, library skills classes may be taught, and there may even be an information literacy curriculum. However, there is no attempt to foster closer relationships between school library media specialist and teacher; information literacy skills and strategies in the school library media center are taught in isolation. This pattern of instruction may even become institutionalized, so that the school library media specialist repetitively teaches certain skills automatically at certain times to certain classes. This instruction may not be synchronized with classroom activities and needs. This level of service can seem quite comfortable, but it may be dangerous. While not as obviously isolated, the school library media specialist is often not accepted as a full member of the educational community, and opportunities to contribute to student information literacy skills in conjunction with other curriculum areas are rare.

Coordination

In the next level, the school library media specialist deliberately works to find out what is happening in individual classrooms. Based on information gained, the school library media specialist may regularly supply a variety of materials, websites, and bibliographies that support the units. Information literacy instruction in the media center can now complement classroom units. While teachers and the school library media specialist are still working separately, at least student information-literacy instruction in the school library media center is more closely aligned with classroom curriculum. While the school library media specialist is now a more active participant in the school community, and may even be valued by other teachers, there is no full understanding or acceptance of the vital role a school library media specialist can fulfill in the curriculum.

Collaboration

In the ultimate level of involvement, the school library media specialist is actively collaborating with teachers throughout the school, involved in planning lessons, units, and the curriculum itself. The school library media specialist is viewed as a full, valued partner by teachers and administrators, and everyone is involved in integrating information-literacy skills throughout the curriculum. Teachers and the school library media specialist regularly meet and plan for student instruction, deliver the lessons and units in both the classroom and school library media center, and actively evaluate students. When appropriate, both professionals are present for one or more lessons, which facilitates communication about lesson content, eliminates unnecessary duplication of material covered, and impresses upon students the complementary teaching roles of all professionals participating in teaching the unit. Ongoing evaluation of each collaborative lesson or unit enables everyone involved to continue to implement quality instruction to students. Furthermore, as Violet H. Harada notes, this level of collaboration is not limited to short-term issues. Instead, "teams must focus on long-term results. In this process, curriculum must be viewed as holistic and dynamic rather than as static and linear."[10] In attaining this level of involvement, the school library media specialist is fulfilling his/her full potential as teacher and information literacy expert. Students are benefiting from the expertise and cooperation of all teachers, and the school library media specialist becomes an essential part of the school community.

REALITY

Collaboration between school library media specialists and teachers can result in benefits for everyone involved — students, teachers, school library media specialists, administrators, and the community overall. At the same time, just as in many other areas, full collaboration all the time with all teachers on all units is not possible. It would take too much time and require too many resources — such as one school library media specialist for every teacher in the school. Also, the school library media specialist has an obligation to develop and maintain a school library media center that supports and enhances school activities.

Instead, the school library media specialist should strive to develop collaborative relationships with all or almost all of the teachers in the school. Through careful management of time and resources, every student in the school should be able to benefit from collaborative teacher/school library media specialist units on a regular basis. (This does not mean daily contact, and indeed may mean only once or twice a semester.) This is important because, as the research shows, students in schools with a professional school library media specialist (especially one working with teachers) achieve higher scores on standardized tests. (See the appendix.)

CONCLUSION

School library media specialists cannot assume that this type of collaboration will simply happen, and often it is not happening. In 1994, Linda Lachance Wolcott reviewed research in this area, and concluded, "Studies have consistently reached the same conclusion: with few exceptions, school library media specialists are not involved in instructional planning."[11] There are usually a variety of reasons why school library media specialists do not collaborate more, and some of them are within the greater school environment. Many administrators truly do not understand what school library media specialists can contribute to student learning or that school library media centers are important components of the educational experience for students. Teachers often do not perceive school library media specialists as potential partners with significant contributions to make in the design and implementation and evaluation of lessons. Often this is not because of antagonism: Many administrators and classroom teachers simply do not know what skills and training the school library media specialist possesses and how that training could contribute to student education. In many elementary schools, the school library media specialist provides mandated "prep" or planning time for teachers. In some high schools, study hall is scheduled in the school library media center; in others, so many study-hall students gravitate to the more inviting space of the school library media center that it is difficult for the school library media specialist to work with teachers and classes. Given this lack of understanding of the vital role of the school library media specialist in schools, school library media specialists must be proactive, reach out from the school library media center, and actively educate others in the school about the role and value of the school library media specialist in the curriculum—and they must do this without antagonizing their fellow professionals.

NOTES

1. American Association of School Librarians and Association for Educational Communications and Technology, *Information Power: Building Partnerships for Learning* (Chicago: American Library Association, 1998), 103.

2. American Association of School Librarians and Association for Educational Communications and Technology, *Information Power*, 104.

3. Keith Curry Lance, "What Research Tells Us about the Importance of School Libraries," (paper included in the proceedings of the White House Conference on School Libraries, Tuesday, June 4, 2002), 20.

4. American Association of School Librarians and Association for Educational Communications and Technology, *Information Power*, 1.

5. Carol C. Kuhlthau, "The Process of Learning from Information," *School Libraries Worldwide* 1, no. 1 (1995), 2.

6. *Webster's New World Dictionary of the American Language* (New York: World, 1966), 286.

7. Marshall Welch, "Collaboration as a Tool for Inclusion," in *Inclusive Education: A Casebook and Readings for Prospective and Practicing Teachers*, ed. Suzanne E. Wade (Mahwah, N.J.: L. Erlbaum Associates, 2000), 73.

8. Linda Corey, "The Role of the Library Media Specialist in Standards-Based Learning," *Knowledge Quest* 31, no. 2 (November/December 2002), 21.

9. Jean Donham, "Collaboration in the Media Center: Building Partnerships for Learning," *NASSP Bulletin* 83, no. 605 (March 1999), 21.

10. Violet H. Harada, "Taking the Lead in Developing Learning Communities." *Knowledge Quest* 31, no. 2 (November/December 2002), 13.

11. Linda Lachance Wolcott, "Understanding How Teachers Plan: Strategies for Successful Instructional Partnerships," *School Library Media Quarterly* 22, no. 3 (Spring 1994), 161.

CHAPTER 2

Collaboration in the School

It is important for the school library media specialist to collaborate with other teachers in the school. However, the type of rich, multifaceted collaboration described in chapter 1 does not just happen by itself. In an article discussing the role of collaboration in the business world, Andy Moore remarks, "Collaborative environments are not automatic. They do not emerge, fully successful."[1] This is true about the environment for collaboration within schools, also. Often, the role of the school library media specialist in the school is misunderstood. Furthermore, many teachers and administrators do not fully understand the value of collaboration. Therefore, the school library media specialist must always be ready to educate others about the value of the school library media center and be willing to initiate collaboration with other professionals.

Research also indicates that collaboration is not a common pattern of interaction in schools. Lawrence Leonard and Pauline Leonard published results of an interpretive survey of 45 teachers in North Louisiana schools: "While many schools have creatively juggled schedules and identified additional resources that are used to occasionally free up teachers for shared work, many have not."[2] This means that a school library media specialist may be able to work with teachers who are already collaborating, or that the specialist may need to initiate collaboration in the school.

In reality, there are several patterns of interaction among administrators, teachers, and school library media specialists that can occur. Some teachers and administrators will have had positive experiences with school library media specialists, perhaps even opportunities to collaborate with them. When this is the case, prior experience can predispose the teachers and administrators to favor the collaboration sought by the school library media specialist. At the same time, many members of the school community have had little or no experience collaborating with school library media specialists; nevertheless, it should not be assumed that they are opposed to the idea of collaborating with the school library media specialist. Unfortunately, some teachers and administrators have had very bad experiences with school library media specialists in their past, which makes it harder to establish collaboration in the school. In rare cases, school library media specialists are collaborating regularly with the entire staff, under the leadership of the school administration. However, indifference or antagonism are often the norm, and this means the school library media specialist must be ready to develop and execute a plan to promote collaboration within his or her school.

ADMINISTRATORS AND THEIR ROLES IN COLLABORATION

In a recent research project, Debra Lau surveyed school administrators to document their perceptions of the school library media center:

> Eight out of ten of the principals surveyed say they strongly believe the media center plays a positive role in the overall value of the school. But when asked to back up that statement, only 47 percent say there's a direct link between an effective media center and increased student achievement, and just 41 percent say the school library has a positive impact on students' standardized test scores.[3]

(See the appendix for a review of the literature supporting the role of the school library media specialist in student achievement and in information literacy overall.)

This is especially unfortunate, since the school administration is vitally important to the success or failure of collaboration within any individual school. The principal can support the idea of collaboration, oppose it, or be indifferent to it. In speaking about districtwide implementation of mental health services between external agencies and public schools, Jeanne Jehl and Michael W. Kirst address the role of principals in helping the endeavor be successful. The principal "must be an active participant, . . . serve as an advocate, . . . reorganize and link key teachers and other staff, . . . [and] act as an 'enabler.'"[4] Rochelle B. Senator notes that administrators can support collaboration through providing a common planning time, through the way the schedule is designed, through encouraging teachers to participate in collaboration with the school library media specialist, and by providing staff development time.[5] David Sanders is a principal, and he directly states, "The principal should establish the expectation that the [school library media specialist] will participate in and conduct actual class-room instructional lessons. This puts the [school library media special-ist] in a place where his or her instructional expertise can be demon-strated to the classroom teachers and lends credibility to the process."[6]

Given this pivotal role for the principal as facilitator and endorser, the school library media specialist should work to establish a good working relationship with the principal and other administrators and should use it as a basis for fostering collaboration with the teachers within the school. In speaking of administrators and teachers, Gary N. Hartzell notes that "many, perhaps most, of them do not understand the value and educational potential of libraries and librarians. It isn't that they don't like them, and they certainly aren't out to 'get 'em.' Mostly, it's just a matter of indifference."[7] So, in building support for collabo-ration, the school library media specialist will need to educate the prin-cipal about the role and the potential value to be gained from having a fully involved school library media specialist in the school. (Studies cited in the appendix report research showing that in schools where the school library media specialist collaborates with teachers, student achievement test scores are higher than in schools without such collab-oration.) Some experts suggest that the school library media specialist might be more successful in working with an assistant principal, who may have fewer responsibilities and be more open to new ideas. Each school library media specialist must work within the climate of the in-dividual school and determine which administrator would be best to work with, when there is a choice.

The search for administrative support can begin with the job inter-view. School library media specialists can use such opportunities to ask administrators to discuss their perceptions of the role of the library media specialist in the school. The administrator's responses can often indicate whether the principal is antagonistic to a proactive, collaborative role for the school library media specialist, indifferent to such a role, or truly supportive. The school library media specialist can also take the opportunity to discuss a desire to work collaboratively with teaching faculty of the school. Such interactions can help the school library media specialist determine whether it is possible to participate fully in and support any collaborative efforts currently in the school, or even to assume a leadership role in developing or extending collaboration in the school.

In cases where the administration is antagonistic or indifferent, the school library media specialist must begin to educate the principal or assistant principal about the value of collaboration. One place to begin is by sharing *Information Power: Building Partnerships for Learning* with the administrators. These 1998 national standards present strong arguments for the collaborative role of the school library media specialist in the educational setting. The fact that this role for the school library media specialist is presented and advocated by the American Association of School Librarians (AASL) can be useful. In addition to providing a personal copy of these standards for each administrator, the media specialist may wish to share "An Overview of *Information Power: Building Partnerships for Learning*." This brief (three-page) article is the result of a class assignment given to Educational Media students, to "simplify, clarify, and succinctly report" the content of the new national standards.[8] This article is more readily accessible than the full-length book, which exceeds two hundred pages in length; busy administrators may find it is a good introduction to the role of the school library media specialist in the school community. The school library media specialist can reinforce any impressions gleaned by the administrator with follow-up information and discussion.

Media specialists need to articulate the AASL definition of information literacy and also their specialized knowledge in this area. Administrators and others in the school community need to understand the extent of this expertise and the role information literacy should play in the school's curriculum. It may also be necessary to remind people that a school library media specialist is also a teacher, not merely a guardian of books. Formal presentations at faculty meetings or PTO/PTA meetings or during in-service training can be carefully planned to showcase school library media specialist skills. Also, informal conversation, a school library media center website or newsletter, and annotated bibliographies of materials can all be used to further explain or highlight information literacy. Each school library media specialist must use whatever resources are available to communicate with the school community. School library media specialists' work to educate both education professionals and the general public about their knowledge of and expertise in information literacy and instructional design should be ongoing; it will not be finished quickly. But a widespread understanding of this expertise is the necessary foundation for collaboration.

While working to educate administrators and the greater educational community, the school library media specialist should identify teachers, perhaps two, who are receptive to the idea of collaboration and actually develop and implement a jointly planned lesson or unit with them. One of the most effective ways to convince others to participate in and support collaboration among teachers and the school library media specialist is actually to demonstrate the benefits. This shows that what works in theory and in other schools can also work in your school, with your students. Furthermore, the teachers who are involved will likely press for the opportunity to work together with the school library media specialist again; such support is valuable.

There are also schools where the idea of collaboration is accepted but where the potential role of the school library media specialist in collaboration is unfamiliar. In these cases, the school library media specialist needs to indicate desire and willingness to participate in collaborative activities. When given an opportunity to be part of a group working collaboratively, the school library media specialist needs to work within the norms already established by the group, concentrating on becoming part of the current system instead of trying to assume a leadership role.

It may take time to gain administrative support for an active, involved role for the school library media specialist in the school. It is time well spent, and the process cannot be rushed. The school library media specialist needs to use effective people skills and acquire personal knowledge of the administrator's style in order to build support for an active, involved role for the school library media specialist. It is counterproductive to be so insistent or aggressive that the administrator becomes indifferent or (in the worst case) antagonistic.

In some schools, collaboration among personnel is accepted and well integrated into the climate of the school. Often, in these cases, the administration is supportive of collaboration, and the principal or assistant principal publicly endorses or enables it. It will be easier for the school library media specialist to foster and participate in collaboration activities if it is clear to the school community that the administration supports the idea. This "sign of approval" can give the media specialist credibility.

A skilled administrator can work to promote and enable collaboration in the school in creative ways. For example, in an elementary school, students may have classes outside the regular classroom with specialized teachers in such topics as music, art, and physical education. The principal could schedule these enrichment classes so that students in one grade are occupied in these activities one morning a month, effectively freeing the teachers for an extensive planning session. By creative scheduling or acquisition of grants, it may be possible to arrange for the school library media specialist to join the teachers, in which case collaborative planning could occur during school hours.

Administrators could require teachers to participate in collaborative planning. Some collaboration theorists support this type of mandatory participation;[9] others believe it undermines the collaborative effort.[10] This mandatory approach works in some situations; teachers who are required to participate in collaborative planning may come to believe in and value collaboration with the school library media specialist. However, there may be at least some teachers opposed to collaboration, and they may refuse to participate fully, even while going through the motions. In reality, it may take several years for some teachers to realize fully the benefits of collaboration and become supportive. Other teachers may continue to be adamantly opposed to collaborative planning with the school library media specialist. This can be especially true in schools where classes with the library media specialist are designated as release time for teachers. Donna M. Shannon studied the implementation of flexible scheduling in two elementary schools in Kentucky. She found that "by far, the most serious challenge is related to teacher planning time. The library media specialists in these two schools have traditionally provided a thirty-minute planning time for teachers. Teachers believed that they had 'lost' planning time by moving to a flexible access library program."[11]

In such cases, teachers may mourn and resent for several years the loss of what they perceive as "their" time. There is hope, however, as shown by a teacher who shared this insight with Shannon: "I think that once teachers have collaborated with the school library media specialist, they will see the benefit."[12]

When implemented, mandatory collaboration may be phased in gradually, one subject or grade level at a time, or it may be required of all school personnel at the same time. Everyone involved needs to remember that true collaboration is time-intensive. Finding the time and energy to begin collaboration at once with all teachers in the school and to develop positive relationships with everyone, all at the same time, may be overwhelming for the library media specialist.

The personalities of all the people involved, the leadership style and confidence of the principal, the abilities of the school library media specialist, and the climate of the school can all influence the final outcome of mandatory collaboration. Such an approach can work; I have seen it happen. However, this is not necessarily the easiest or most effective way to implement collaboration. The administrator and the school library media specialist must both be completely committed to this approach, ready to devote the time and resources necessary for success. They must both stand firm against complaints and petitions from classroom teachers to return to the "old" ways of doing things in the school. The individual school library media specialist should be aware of ramifications of mandatory collaboration, and it may be useful to discuss these issues with administrators who suggest or support compulsory participation.

The principal or assistant principal may choose to participate actively in the collaborative meetings between teachers and the media specialist. In such cases, administrators should act as equal participants, not carrying the weight of their formal authority into the meeting. In true collaboration, all individuals participating are perceived to be "equals," with no one individual superior to any other.[13] True collaboration, with the freedom to exchange ideas and knowledge, is hampered when someone in the group holds power over another. Depending on personalities and individual management styles, the school library media specialist may be able to discuss this point with administrators who plan to join the planning sessions.

At the very least, an administrator who is willing to allow the school library media specialist to promote and participate in collaborative planning with teachers is required for success. Even with very limited support (and in the absence of active administrative opposition), the school library media specialist can begin to reach beyond the school library media center and work with one or two teachers. As these early efforts succeed and information about the value of these relationships spreads, others in the school often become more supportive of the idea of collaborating with the school library media specialist and may even express the desire to become involved. While this approach can be slow, it will work. I personally have seen the success of this technique, and many of my students have reported positive results when collaboration is approached in this way.

Eric Bredo studied collaborative teaching efforts in 16 San Francisco Bay–area elementary schools. "The picture of teaching teams that emerges from this study is clear and consistent. The teams are primarily small, voluntaristic, and of equal status."[14] This supports the idea of starting with one or two teachers and of limiting collaborative meetings to individual teachers or to small groups of grade-level teachers or subject specialists. When working on interdisciplinary or intergrade-level projects, it is probably best to limit the number of group members until collaboration is firmly established and fully understood in the school. For example, one seventh-grade teacher and one first-grade teacher could be involved in planning a unit for the adolescents to write and illustrate fairy tales to read to first graders. After one successful implementation of the grade plan, other teachers could be involved, or the school library media specialist could do the same lesson a second or third time for additional interested teachers.

It is an unfortunate fact that some administrators are totally opposed to the idea of a school library media specialist's actively collaborating with teachers and helping to integrate information literacy throughout the curriculum. If this attitude becomes apparent during the job interview, a school library media specialist dedicated to working collaboratively would be advised to find another job. If already committed to the school, the best approach may be to try to determine reasons for the administrator's opposition and, on the basis of this information, try to educate him or her about the positive effects a proactive school library media specialist could have on student learning. (Many of the articles included in the review of the literature in the appendix can provide information about the role and value of school library media specialists in the school.) Most educators are truly concerned about the students in the school; however, some administrators are not approachable and will not change. In these rare cases, school library media specialists must do the best they can under difficult conditions.

Summary

- *Inform them about the role of the school library media specialist in the school.*
- *Ask questions in the job interview to gauge their knowledge or support.*
- *Share Information Power: Building Partnerships for Learning.*
- *Identify a supportive administrator who:*

  - *Indicates approval of school library media specialist involvement in collaboration*
  - *Uses creative scheduling to allow time for collaboration*
  - *May or may not choose to mandate collaboration*
  - *May or may not choose to participate in collaboration.*

- *Even without active support, if there is not administrative opposition to school library media specialist collaboration, begin to work with individual teachers.*

TEACHERS AND COLLABORATION

The school library media specialist must realize that most teachers will not come to the school library media center seeking a partner for collaborative planning. Even if collaboration is already an accepted part of teaching within the school, most teachers are likely to look for partners among their grade-level or department colleagues. Michael Bell and Herman L. Totten studied professional personnel in elementary schools. They conclude, "Most research continues to show low levels of instructional cooperation in general between library media specialists and classroom teachers."[15] So, the school library media specialist must be proactive in creating opportunities to collaborate with teachers.

Ray Doiron and Judy Davies have written on how school library media specialists and teachers can work together to enhance student learning. One strength of their book is the authors' extensive personal experience in school library media centers. They have identified these characteristics of collaboration:

- Collaborative planning and teaching is a process.
- For school library media specialists, collaborative planning and teaching is the *pervasive* method; for teachers, it is an *alternative* method.
- Each partner in the process has expertise to bring to the collaboration.
- The process is focused on developing student-centered activities "that are facilitated, monitored, and evaluated by both the classroom teacher and the teacher librarian."[16]

Their comments both support a role for school library media specialists in the teaching process, and they give guidance as to how to proceed.

Teacher Resistance to Collaboration

Generally, the school library media specialist finds that at least some teachers are reluctant to participate in collaboration. While exploring the potential for school–community relations, Robert L. Crowson and William Lowe Boyd list a number of issues that may hinder collaboration, including professional isolation, "turf" considerations, facility barriers, and procedural restrictions.[17] While their comments are focused on the idea of teachers working with those from outside the school, they make some valid points.

Role of School Library Media Specialist

Teachers may resist because they do not understand the role the school library media specialist can play in integrating information-literacy skills into the school curriculum. There can be a variety of reasons for their lack of knowledge about the role of the school library media specialist:

- They may not remember or realize that the school library media specialist has experience in teaching.
- They are not aware of the school library media specialist's expertise in both information literacy and in instructional design, which enables the school library media specialist to share that expertise with students.
- They may have had bad experiences with a school library media specialist in the past.

Isolation

In some schools, the teachers are used to working alone in their self-contained classrooms and the school library media specialist works alone in the media center—both being forms of professional isolation. Such isolation can result in the idea of "turf" belonging to one individual, who is in control within that classroom or center. The concept of sharing ideas and responsibilities in a collaborative lesson may be both unfamiliar and intimidating. It is often easier to initiate collaboration in schools where teachers are already involved with team teaching or collaboration. Where there is some resistance, it may be effective to work initially with one or two willing teachers and let successful collaborations entice other teachers to become involved.

Time

Another reason that teachers may resist the idea of collaboration with the school library media specialist is the issue of time. Because of school procedures or limited facilities, it can be difficult for educators to find a time or place to work together. As we all know, in today's schools, teachers are overwhelmed by record keeping, in addition to teaching their students. When approached about working with the school library media specialist to design and deliver instruction, the teacher may feel that it will not be possible to find the time needed, especially if there is no time during the school day for collaborative planning. This attitude does not imply antagonism or even unwillingness; any additional effort may simply seem overwhelming. This means the school library media specialist must prove to the teachers that collaboration is indeed worth the time and effort put into it.

One approach that can be effective is to provide individual teachers with traditional school library media center services. Suggesting resources appropriate to a specific unit or offering to teach a specific library or information literacy skill can initiate a professional relationship. The school library media specialist can continue these types of activities while suggesting more collaborative work too.

Time for collaboration can also be an issue for the school library media specialist. In a study of elementary school library media specialists, Jean Donham van Deusen noted factors that influenced how they used available time. "Automated circulation, available paid support staff, class scheduling pattern, and assignment to a single building are all factors that gave the library media specialist more time. Time saved appeared to be used, at least in part, to provide services to teachers."[18] Among the documented services to teachers was an increase in "consultation activities," a part of collaboration as defined here.

In spite of the reality of lack of time to collaborate, the research provides some encouraging evidence. Marshall Welch and Beth Tulbert did an extensive literature review on collaboration theory in the education literature, identified several factors they deemed vital for collaboration, and asked practitioners about their perceptions of the influence of each of them on effective collaboration. "Finding time to collaborate is often a problem facing educators. Despite this, results from this investigation do not suggest that time was a major factor. This result suggests that practitioners who value collaboration somehow manage to find time for it, especially if they have routine locations and facilitators to coordinate meetings."[19] This suggests that lack of time, in and of itself, does not stop collaboration where teachers and school library media specialists are committed to it.

Resources

Resources available to the school library media specialist and the teachers can either negatively or positively affect willingness to collaborate. While Friend and Cook indicate that those who truly collaborate share their resources,[20] the presence or absence of time, money, space, or knowledge can help or hinder collaboration. Time to work together is one such resource, as addressed above. Money can be another: Making funding available to purchase materials or equipment to support lessons that are designed collaboratively can be a way to reward teachers who are willing to collaborate. These funds might be provided by supportive administrators, or the school library media specialist and teachers can obtain grants for one-time startup money or for materials. The school library media specialist may be able to earmark money in the collection-development budget for curriculum support.

At the same time, teachers who have resources or funds in their classrooms may not be willing to share them. In this case, the best course of action may be to accept the teacher's decision to not share and continue with the collaboration. With time, the evidence of other successful collaborations in the school, and occasionally the intervention of the administrator, may make these teachers more willing to pool resources and become full participants in the collaboration process.

The knowledge and training of the teachers and the school library media specialist are additional resources. The teachers have subject-area expertise, and the school library media specialist has training in information literacy. Both teachers and the school library media specialist know how to teach, and both have experience with the students in the school. Cooperative sharing of this background and learning results in stronger, more varied lessons. Even those in knowledge management acknowledge this principle. "People still need people, and fully formed strategies are almost always better served *en masse*."[21]

Space

Space is another resource to consider when planning collaboratively. Some schools are very crowded, with little space available for planning or for instruction. Often, teachers and media specialists will plan a unit together and decide what the teacher will teach and what the media specialist will teach. Teachers will then instruct their students in their own classrooms. Sometimes, it is also possible to bring classes to the school library media center. In some schools so many classes are scheduled in the library media center that it is difficult to find time for collaborative teaching there. It is helpful if the school library media specialist can be in the classroom with the teacher for at least part of a collaborative unit. This sends the message to students that the school library media specialist is a teacher too, and it may signal acceptance by the teacher of the partnership. This is especially useful when collaboration is first beginning in the school, since students do not always understand this role either and are unclear about what the school library media specialist can contribute to their education. Also, it can be very helpful to the school library media specialist to know firsthand what the teacher has told the students before they go to the school library media center to complete an assignment. In the ideal situation, the school library media specialist and the teacher use the classroom and the media center both jointly and separately, depending on who is teaching what to how many students at any particular time.

Benefits of Collaboration

In spite of the obstacles common in schools, collaboration is indeed worth the effort. Students will benefit from exposure to the skills, ideas, and energy of two or more people. Multiple inputs can result in more variety in teaching methods, as ideas and experiences and suggestions are shared. Students have the opportunity to learn from at least two different people. Both the teachers and the school library media specialist have more options for presenting instruction, because there is more flexibility for grouping students when two or more adults are available to work with them.

Another benefit is that collaborative efforts to teach information literacy are often more successful than individual, isolated efforts by either the school library media specialist or the teacher. Research has shown that when library skills (also known as *information literacy skills*) are integrated into the curriculum, better learning occurs and students are more likely to retain and later use these skills. (See the appendix for references to research studies on this topic, specifically

Eisenberg & Brown, the Michigan Department of Education, the American Association of School Librarians, Haycock, Todd, Hartzell, and Kearney.) Furthermore, evidence from the national Library Power project indicates that collaboration between teachers and school library media specialists results in less isolated teaching of library skills. "The final conclusion was that, in the units reported, library skills were not often isolated in the library, but instead were essential to student success in attaining curriculum unit objectives."[22]

Summary

- *Media specialists must proactively seek collaboration with teachers.*
- *Possible sources of teacher resistance to collaboration:*

  - *Don't understand role and training of media specialist*
  - *Used to working alone*
  - *Don't have time.*

- *Factors to inhibit/support collaboration:*

  - *Resources*
  - *Time (need to show collaboration is worth the effort)*
  - *Money (may be able to find funds)*
  - *Knowledge and expertise of both teachers and media specialists*
  - *Space (can share both classroom and media center areas).*

- *Benefits include integration of information-literacy skills into the broader curriculum.*

CONCLUSION

It is important to remember that most of the people working in schools are there because they want to work with and help the children and young adults who are their students. Most teachers and administrators truly want to do what is best for their students. This means that school library media specialists, teachers, and administrators have a common goal. Building on this common goal gives the school library media specialist a basis for promoting collaboration in the school.

NOTES

1. Andy Moore, "Is there a Doctrinaire in the House?" Special supplement to *KM World* (March 2003), S3.

2. Lawrence Leonard and Pauline Leonard, "The Continuing Trouble with Collaboration: Teachers Talk," *Current Issues in Education* 6, no. 15 (2003), 10, 14, cie.ed.asu.edu/volume6/number15/ (Accessed February 9, 2004).

3. Bulleted list extracted from Debra Lau, "What Does Your Boss Think about You?" *School Library Journal* 48, no. 9 (September 2002), 52.

4. Jeanne Jehl and Michael W. Kirst, "Getting Ready to Provide School-Linked Services: What Schools Must Do," *Education and Urban Society* 25, no. 2 (February 1993), 160–161.

5. Rochelle B. Senator, *Collaboration for Literacy: Creating an Integrated Language Arts Program for Middle Schools* (Westport, Conn.: Greenwood, 1995), 145–148.

6. David Sanders, "A Principal's Perspective," *Knowledge Quest* 31, no. 2 (November/December 2002), 31.

7. Gary N. Hartzell, "The Invisible School Librarian," *Knowledge Quest* 31, no. 2 (November/December 2002), 25.

8. Students in the Educational Media Masters Program, University of Central Florida, "An Overview of *Information Power: Building Partnerships for Learning*," *Knowledge Quest* 27 (January/February 1999), 14–16.

9. Marilyn Friend and Lynne Cook, *Interactions: Collaboration Skills for School Professionals*, 2nd ed. (White Plains, N.Y.: Longman, 1996), 7.

10. Beth Doll et al., "Cohesion and Dissension in a Multi-Agency Family Service Team: A Qualitative Examination of Service Integration," *Children's Services: Social Policy, Research, and Practice* 3, no. 1 (2000), 4.

11. Donna M. Shannon, "Tracking the Transition to a Flexible Access Library Program in Two Library Power Elementary Schools," *School Library Media Quarterly* 24, no. 3 (Spring 1996), 159.

12. Shannon, "Tracking the Transition to a Flexible Access Library Program in Two Library Power Elementary Schools," 159.

13. Friend and Cook, *Interactions*, 7.

14. Eric Bredo, "Collaborative Relations among Elementary School Teachers," *Sociology of Education* 50, no. 4 (October 1977), 306.

15. Michael Bell and Herman L. Totten, "Cooperation in Instruction between Classroom Teachers and School Library Media Specialists," *School Library Media Quarterly* 20, no. 2 (Winter 1992), 83.

16. Ray Doiron and Judy Davies, *Partners in Learning: Students, Teachers, and the School Library* (Englewood, Colo.: Libraries Unlimited, 1998), 23.

17. Robert L. Crowson and William Lowe Boyd, "Coordinated Services for Children: Designing Arks for Storms and Seas Unknown," *American Journal of Education* 101, no. 2 (February 1993), 143.

18. Jean Donham van Deusen, "An Analysis of the Time Use of Elementary School Library Media Specialists and Factors that Influence It," *School Library Media Quarterly* 24, no. 2 (Winter 1996), 90.

19. Marshall Welch and Beth Tulbert, "Practitioners' Perspectives of Collaboration: A Social Validation and Factor Analysis," *Journal of Educational and Psychological Consultation* 11, nos. 3 and 4 (2000), 371.

20. Friend and Cook, *Interactions*, 9.

21. Peter J. Auditore, "The Many Faces of Collaboration," Special Supplement to *KMWorld* (March 2003), S4.

22. Norman L. Webb and Carol A. Doll, "Contributions of Library Power to Collaborations between Librarians and Teachers," *School Libraries Worldwide* 5, no. 2 (1999), 37.

CHAPTER 3

Collaborating with Teachers

The ultimate goal for the school library media specialist is an active school library media program where collaboration with teachers is accepted and information literacy skills are fully incorporated throughout the curriculum. As stated in chapter 2, it is not possible to collaborate fully and completely with every teacher on every lesson. However, it is possible to incorporate a pattern of collaboration across the school, involving all teachers and all students. Such a result does not occur spontaneously or easily. Instead, the media specialist must carefully reach out to and develop positive relationships with administrators and teachers. This chapter suggests some ways to approach that task.

FIRST STEPS

The school library media specialist should first get to know the teachers, administrators, and culture of the school itself. School library media specialists going into a new school (either as a new school library media specialist or because of a change in jobs) may take the entire first year to learn about the new environment. It takes time to understand the culture of the school, learn about its curriculum, figure out the administrator's preferred management style, connect with individual teachers in the school, and generally become acquainted with the setting in which everyone will be working. This does not mean that the school library media specialist does nothing for the first year; it means that the school library media specialist takes the time to learn the new culture before making major changes that could cause resistance, if not actual antagonism.

Some professionals believe that it is more beneficial for school library media specialists to initiate changes in and through the center quickly, to take advantage of their "new" status. If school personnel seem to expect new policies, procedures, and interactions with the media center, this could be appropriate. However, any changes made must work within and through the culture of the school.

While working to understand the environment, the school library media specialist can start to educate administrators about the role of the school library media program in the school and initiate planning with them for future school library media center programs. Keep in mind that not all administrators see the school library media specialist as a key component in curricular support; even minimal increases in their awareness would be useful. While it is easier to implement collaboration with teachers with administrative support than without it, lack of support does not make it impossible to develop collaborative relationships with teachers on an individual basis.

By taking the time to understand fully the culture of the school environment, the new school library media specialist is less likely to inadvertently make decisions that annoy users, such as discarding the disreputable-looking book that is used by the first-grade teacher each year to teach the term *spectacles* to young students. Also, throughout this introductory year, the school library media specialist can lay the groundwork and build support for potentially controversial policies that enhance school library media center services, such as requiring elementary teachers to stay with their classes during library period.

Interviewing school library media specialists, Shirley Weisman identified keys to successful collaboration:

- Have a clear picture of what you want to teach and also know the curricular standards for your school
- Be persistent in advocating the value of collaboration
- Reach out to people who need your help the most
- Remember that collaboration happens more easily in settings with schoolwide or districtwide collaboration.[1]

During this first year, the school library media specialist may use any and all traditional service strategies to bring the school library media center to the attention of individual teachers. Conversations in the teacher's lounge can give the school library media specialist information about classroom units. A monthly newsletter or weekly e-mails can highlight a wide variety of things, including new items acquired for the school library media center, recommended websites, bibliographies for specific topics, and other announcements. The school library media specialist could share new materials at faculty meetings. A form could be developed for teachers to indicate units they are teaching so the school library media specialist can pull together materials to support classroom instruction. Occasional offerings of coffee and cookies in the school library media center can entice teachers and administrators to visit. It is also appropriate to offer to help teachers with lessons, display student work in the school library media center, or develop a display that complements classroom activities. A school library media center website also raises visibility, especially if it includes links useful for teachers, for administrators, and even for students. Any and all efforts to reach out to and support classroom teachers begin to lay groundwork for more formal, intensive collaboration.

This initial year also gives the school library media specialist time to know the other professionals in the school, form friendships, and get a feeling for the social and political structure. At the same time, the other professionals have the opportunity to get to know the school library media specialist. All members of the school community benefit from these chances to build professional relationships.

Occasionally, individuals who have been working as classroom teachers earn library and information science master's degrees and become library media specialists in the same school where they have worked as classroom teachers. Such school library media specialists have some specific advantages in establishing collaboration. First, the teachers and administrators and students already know them, and they already know the individuals in the school. This can significantly shorten the work needed to understand the culture of the school and to build working relationships. The new school library media specialist also knows how teachers, students, and administrators felt about and worked with the former school library media specialist; this knowledge can provide invaluable information while the "newbie" works either to sustain or change those impressions and feelings. Also, other teachers are more likely to accept the school library media specialist in the role of fellow teacher (which is vital to successful collaboration), since that individual *was* a teacher in the school.

Summary

- *Get to know the administrators, teachers, students, curriculum, school culture, and school politics.*
- *Publicize the school library media center and its collections and activities:*

  - *Send monthly newsletter or e-mail messages*
  - *Bring new materials to faculty meetings*
  - *Create and use a form indicating future curriculum units*
  - *Provide coffee and cookies in the school library media center*
  - *Display student work*
  - *Create and maintain a school library media center website.*

- *Individuals who become school library media specialists in the same school where they taught have unique advantages.*

BEGINNING COLLABORATION

Once the school library media specialist has become acquainted with the school itself and the professionals who work there, it is time to begin actively advocating for full collaboration with one or more teachers. This can be done in a number of ways: discussing the value of collaboration; volunteering to provide materials, space, or expertise; actually working with one or more teachers to model collaboration; and sharing information from the professional literature. Also, it is important to remember that not every teacher will be involved in collaboration with the school library media specialist for all classroom activities.

The school library media specialist should remember that the style of collaboration described here is revolutionary and that schools in general are often slow to accept major change. Many educators are familiar with and comfortable with the traditional role for school library media specialists—that of providers of materials to support classroom instruction and teachers of library skills. It takes time and patience to change this limited perception.

In those rare cases where there is full administrative support, collaboration may already be initiated for the whole school. In that case, the administrator often arranges for the school library media specialist and teachers to meet and plan instruction for lessons or units. An entire new procedure and pattern for planning time may be needed. It can be very difficult to implement and support a change of this magnitude without sufficient funds for release time, planning time, training, and materials. Even with full administrative support, it is often best to start with one department or grade level and, once collaboration is well established there, integrate other grades or subjects. The results, showing the benefits to both teachers and students, can be used to encourage other educators to become involved.

In most instances, the school library media specialist will be working with a teacher or teachers who volunteer for, or who agree to try, collaboration when approached by the school library media specialist. In schools where team or departmental planning already exists, it is probably easier for the school library media specialist to find a willing partner or partners. In schools with isolated, self-contained classrooms, this may be more difficult; however, it is not impossible. Even in these more "traditional" schools, some educators are willing to try something different, especially if there is the potential to improve instruction and student learning through collaboration.

The school library media specialist needs to avoid the appearance of favoritism in selecting initial volunteers. The idea of collaboration with teachers could be presented as a school library media program goal, with the ultimate objective being to collaborate with everyone. Based on this type of plan, it may be useful to develop a systematic approach and to work with grade levels or departments in a sequential manner.

The school library media specialist should use professional judgment and knowledge of individual teachers to identify a particular person to approach for the first collaborative project. This may be a teacher who has been a mentor to the school library media specialist. It may be the teacher who is more open to new ideas and teaching techniques. It may be the teacher presenting a unit for the first time. It may be the teacher who is beginning a unit on a subject of personal or professional interest to the school library media specialist. It may be the teacher who is a leader in the school. Based on research in elementary schools, Michael Bell and Herman L. Totten stress the need for the school library media specialist to build a positive relationship with "recognized instructional leaders on the faculty who may be, as suggested by these findings, slightly more disposed than the average to cooperate with the library media specialist."[2]

Either a quiet, individualistic approach or a very public planned approach that includes everyone can be appropriate. The school library media specialist must use professional knowledge of the situation and the people involved to determine how to handle the initial approach. If there is strong opposition to the whole idea, a quiet approach aimed at proving its value can be used as a basis for a later publicized plan incorporating everyone. It is extremely important for school library media specialists to remember that their role is to provide materials and services (including participation in collaborative planning) to *everyone* in the school—not just selected individuals.

Once the method of approach has been identified, the next step is to ask people to participate in a jointly designed project. This invitation may be oral, e-mailed, or written. An oral interaction often implies that an immediate answer is sought. A written or e-mailed request gives the recipients time to think about the offer and its implications before responding. Any e-mail or written announcement should also indicate how soon a response is needed. If an invitation is issued to the entire school community, another announcement should be posted when a volunteer is selected. This is a good time to remind school personnel that everyone will eventually have a chance to participate. Also, teachers may be more or less willing to participate depending on current classroom or personal commitments. Lack of interest from one person now does not mean that person would not be interested at a later date.

Summary

- *Identify a teacher (or teachers) for initial collaboration with the school library media specialist. This person may be a:*

- ○ *Volunteer*
- ○ *Mentor*
- ○ *Teacher starting a new unit*
- ○ *Innovator, willing to try new things*
- ○ *Teachers who provide instructional counseling to fellow teachers.*

- • *Invite that teacher to collaborate; the invitation may be:*

- ○ *Oral*
- ○ *Written*
- ○ *An e-mail.*

FIRST MEETINGS

Once a teacher or teachers have agreed to collaborate, the school library media specialist should begin to plan for the first meeting. The partners need a time and place to meet. It may not be possible to meet during the school day, although that would probably be preferred by all involved. Before school or after school are often possible alternatives; they may be less onerous if the professional staff have to be in the school building when students are not in classes. The school library media specialist should be as flexible as possible about a meeting time, especially when trying to initiate collaboration. It is important to make the initial experience as pleasant and rewarding as possible for the teachers.

When working to find a time to meet, the school library media specialist and teacher need to identify a place to meet. If they meet at school, other activities in the building may limit the areas available. If the teacher would be more comfortable in his or her own classroom, the school library media specialist should agree if possible. The school library media center may also be suitable for their meeting. This can be appropriate if the teacher would be comfortable there and if it is possible to work undisturbed. This is not workable, however, if the school library media specialist is expected to help students and teachers who come into the school library media center during that time. In some situations, it may be helpful for the school library media specialist and teacher to meet someplace else in the school, such as an empty classroom, teacher's lounge, conference room, or office. Whatever arrangements are made, they need a place where they can work without interruption for a useful length of time.

Of course, this first meeting is the time to identify the lesson or lessons to be taught. The teacher may be willing to collaborate on only one lesson or part of one unit, especially for initial efforts at collaboration. The subject, length of the unit, number and characteristics of students, materials to support instruction, teaching methods to be used, and forms of evaluation are all parts of the lesson that could potentially be discussed by the school library media specialist and teacher. (It is not necessary to develop fully all details of the instructional event at this first meeting.) However, there are some other elements of the collaboration that may be less familiar to the school library media specialist and the teacher that also need to be addressed.

It can be a good idea for the teacher and the school library media specialist to share briefly their expectations for the collaboration. This can lead to discussion about perceptions each person has about the role of each individual in the partnership. Research by Tushnet and Doll et al. indicates that "crucial to fostering team cohesion is early identification of interlocking roles for team participants, including the contribution each team member will make and the program activities each will implement."[3] Research studies done in Australia indicated that many of the individuals (63 percent) involved in collaboration did not truly perceive their role to be more than one of delivering information—a one-way role. Ideally, those who collaborate understand the need for interactive roles, where all involved actually provide information and are influenced by, and actively use, information provided by other participants.[4]

While the situations of that study dealt with mental health professionals working to establish a working relationship with teachers in public schools and with government workers, the basic findings apply to the collaboration among school library media specialists and teachers. It is not unusual for the teacher to assume that the role of the school library media specialist is merely to provide the materials needed for a unit. This is, of course, a common perception. It is also the traditional role for the school library media specialist, and may be the role most familiar to and comfortable for teachers. However, it is not the only function for the school library media specialist in a collaborative partnership. Also, it should not be assumed that the teacher and the school library media specialist have the same understanding of collaboration and contributions each participant can make. So, one of the important topics for discussion at the first meeting should be an exploration and clarification of the potential roles for the teacher and the school library media specialist in the partnership.

While building a collaborative model, many traditional services need to be continued. It may be that, without a willingness to assume and build on traditional roles, the school library media specialist will not be able to develop collaboration. However, while engaged in traditional activities, the media specialist should be fully aware of the gap between his or her understanding of the collaboration and that of the teachers'. An initial discussion of the perceived roles of each can be used to help teachers realize that school library media specialists can indeed offer more than just information.

Unless a lengthy meeting is scheduled, a clarification of roles and an initial discussion of the lesson itself may be sufficient for the first session. Before adjourning, both the school library media specialist and teacher should clearly understand what each one will do before the next meeting. Perhaps the school library media specialist will search for websites on the lesson topic and the teacher will identify sources available in the classroom. Both will think about how to approach and deliver the lesson to students and how to evaluate student learning. Working together, the teacher and the school library media specialist should develop realistic expectations for what each person will do and when they plan to meet again to continue work. Also, any decisions made and tasks assigned need to be recorded and shared with all participants as soon as a clean and accurate copy is available. It may be appropriate for the school library media specialist to design collaboration record sheets to track discussions and decisions.

At the next meeting, the school library media specialist and teacher can share sources, ideas, and thoughts generated so far. Through a mutually supportive, nonthreatening exchange of ideas, they can work to develop and finesse a lesson plan that is richer than either one could develop and deliver alone. Then, each can identify areas of the lesson for which they assume responsibility and work individually to develop the final product. For example, the teacher may assume responsibility for teaching in the classroom the physics and geology of earthquakes. The media specialist will locate appropriate websites about earthquakes and plan the media center lesson to teach students how to locate and evaluate these websites. The media specialist and teacher can work independently to develop their own portions of the lesson and share results with each other through e-mail or school mailboxes.

It may not be necessary to schedule a third meeting for collaboration prior to teaching the lesson. However, if either or both participants would like to schedule additional meetings, there is no reason not to do so. It may be impossible to schedule two meetings prior to teaching the lesson. But, whenever possible, at least two meetings are recommended when collaboration is first beginning in the school.

If the school library media specialist and the teacher have worked together before, and both approach the first meeting with complementary expectations, it is possible to deal with all of the issues and topics in one meeting instead of two. Each school library media specialist needs to proceed based on personal knowledge of the teachers and school environment where the collaboration is occurring. One suggested strategy is given here; it may be necessary to change and adapt to meet the needs and culture of a particular school.

Summary

- *Find a time to meet.*
- *Find a place to meet.*
- *At the first meeting:*

  ○ *Clarify the role of each participant*
  ○ *Have an initial discussion of the lesson*
  ○ *Decide what each person will do before the second meeting.*

- *At the second meeting:*

  - *Share information located so far*
  - *Share ideas and brainstorm to finalize the lesson*
  - *Determine final responsibilities.*

- *Either work independently or meet again, as needed.*

TEACHING THE LESSON AND DEBRIEFING

Once the initial planning and instructional design are done, the next step is to teach the collaborative lesson or unit. Both the teacher and the school library media specialist should be involved. Some or all of the instruction may take place in the classroom; some may occur in the school library media center, if it is available. Ideally, both the teacher and the school library media specialist will be present at least part of the time while the other partner is teaching. This is especially important when the unit is being introduced to the students so both partners know what information was given to the students at that time. It should be clear to students that the teacher and the school library media specialist are full and equal partners in designing, implementing, and evaluating the lesson.

The teacher and school library media specialist may do some whole-class instruction, or they may break the students into smaller groups for certain lessons. Working together to teach the lesson allows the school library media specialist and the teacher to make decisions about teaching the whole class or dividing the students into smaller groups, since there are two instructors involved. There are also two different people to answer student questions and evaluate student learning. This added richness can make it easier for students to learn.

Once the lesson has been taught, there must be some way to evaluate student learning. There are a large number of appropriate evaluation and assessment techniques, and determination of which one or ones will be used is part of the collaborative planning process. Both the teacher and the school library media specialist need to be involved in evaluating student learning. After all, if both are teaching, both need to be assessing student learning. For example, the science teacher could evaluate student learning about the geophysics involved in seismology, which the teacher taught. The media specialist could assess student ability to locate and evaluate the quality of websites, which the school library media specialist taught.

The idea of school library media specialists actually evaluating student learning is not readily accepted by all education professionals. But it must be emphasized that this is *not* a move to take over the role of the teacher. Instead, the school library media specialist is assuming full responsibility for evaluating student learning based on materials taught by the school library media specialist. Part of teaching is the evaluation of student learning; the school library media specialist is a teacher and does teach students. Some school districts now mandate school library media specialists grade students in areas of the curriculum, such as information literacy, assigned to the school library media specialist. Also, it is quite possible that the science teacher would not be as comfortable in determining student ability to evaluate websites as in evaluating student learning in the area of seismology; similarly, school library media specialists are not expected to evaluate student learning in seismology.

Once the lesson is taught and student learning is evaluated, the school library media specialist and the teacher must meet at least once more to evaluate the lesson they designed and taught. They should revisit and evaluate all segments of the lesson, including materials used, teaching methods, and the way student learning was evaluated. At the same time, they should also evaluate the collaboration itself, identifying elements that went well and things they would change next time. Without such an evaluation, teaching and collaboration will not improve—and may not continue.

Summary

- *Teach the lesson, with both the teacher and school library media specialist participating.*
- *Evaluate the students, with both the teacher and school library media specialist participating.*
- *Evaluate the lesson and the collaboration.*

CONCLUSION

Not all lessons require multiple sessions or last for days or weeks. Some lessons may be only one day or one session in length. The school library media specialist and teacher cannot collaborate fully on each and every lesson taught in the school, unless the school has an equal number of teachers and school library media specialists. But the school library media specialist will be able to work with at least some of the teachers some of the time, and ideally build up to working with all of the teachers at least once during the school year. Also, it is often easier and less time-consuming to work together again on a unit previously developed through successful collaboration. The procedure outlined above suggests elements to be considered in initiating collaboration. Often, the school library media specialist does not need to assume full responsibility for implementing collaboration in a school. However, the school library media specialist is often excluded from collaboration among teachers. While this is usually an inadvertent oversight, each individual school library media specialist should use personal professional judgment about how to begin collaborating with teachers too.

Summary

Based on a study of how to encourage and develop positive partnerships between schools and home, Ian M. Evans, Akiko Okifuji, and Allison D. Thomas created a list of practical suggestions to follow in enhancing home–school relationships.[5] The following list is modeled on their work:

- *Provide workshops for teachers and administrators about the value and mechanics of collaboration.*
- *Try to create a variety of ways for collaboration to occur between the school library media specialist and teachers—lessons with limited focus or units that may last a semester. It may also be necessary to start from the traditional role of provider of materials and library skills lessons and move to full collaboration in small steps.*
- *Encourage small groups of teachers to work with the school library media specialist. This is one area where the administrator can play a key role.*
- *Identify those teachers least likely to want to collaborate with the school library media specialist and provide some incentive for them to*

do so. This may be making money available to purchase materials to support collaborative units or sharing research results showing that when the school library media specialist is actively collaborating with teachers, student achievement test scores rise.

- *Use small grants to fund materials for collaborative units or release time for teachers and school library media specialist to plan together.*
- *Establish a system to arbitrate conflicts between professionals trying to collaborate together (See chapter 5).*
- *Work to educate teachers and administrators about the role and value of the school library media specialist as an information-literacy expert in the school. Help all to understand that collaboration can help integrate information literacy skills in the school curriculum.*
- *A technique to evaluate all collaborations needs to be developed and implemented. Without effective evaluation, collaboration will not become integral to the school curriculum. Also, annual collaboration evaluations by all faculty, administrators, and the school library media specialist can help to identify the strengths and weaknesses of collaboration as it is implemented in the school.*
- *When possible, establish policies that support and extend collaboration.*

NOTES

1. Shirley Weisman, "Wisdom from *Windows*," *Knowledge Quest* 31, no. 2 (November/December 2002), 32–33.

2. Michael Bell and Herman L. Totten, "Cooperation in Instruction between Classroom Teachers and School Library Media Specialists," *School Library Media Quarterly* 20, no. 2 (Winter 1992), 83.

3. Beth Doll et al., "Cohesion and Dissension in a Multi-Agency Family Service Team: A Qualitative Examination of Service Integration," *Children's Services: Social Policy, Research, and Practice* 3, no. 1 (2000), 2.

4. Richard D. Margerum, "Getting Past Yes: From Capital Creation to Action," *Journal of Planning Literature* 14 (Spring 1999), 187.

5. Ian M. Evans, Akiko Okifuji, and Allison D. Thomas, "Home–School Partnerships: Involving Families in the Educational Process," in *Staying in School: Partnerships for Educational Change*, ed. Ian M. Evans et al. (Baltimore: Paul H. Brookes, 1995), 37–38.

CHAPTER 4

Collaboration Skills

Collaboration is not a solo activity; it cannot occur without two or more people who have agreed to work together. While not absolutely necessary, active administrative support facilitates collaboration by creating an atmosphere that encourages members of the school community to work together. Once a teacher or teachers have agreed to collaborate with the school library media specialist, it is important for the school library media specialist to be aware of interpersonal dynamics before, during, and after the collaborative planning. An awareness of these issues can provide the school library media specialist with insight into the personal interactions during collaboration. This knowledge, and the insights based on it, have the potential to make the school library media specialist a more successful collaborator. This knowledge also helps the school library media specialist protect against teachers who are stonewalling, those who want to take advantage of the situation, or those who pretend to be interested but really are not. Even if the teachers actively collaborate with each other, knowledge of collaboration skills can enable the school library media specialist to work more effectively with them.

ENCOURAGING/ENABLING COLLABORATION

During meetings with a teacher or teachers, there are some factors and issues that tend to encourage the idea of collaboration. Howard S. Adelman notes that appropriate incentives for the proposed change can improve the chance for successful collaboration between mental health agencies and schools.[1] Jeanne Jehl and Michael W. Kirst note that it is mandatory for the team to develop a common mission.[2] Melvin Delgado, in discussing how schools can successfully work with a Puerto Rican community, states, "Failure to understand how all parties can benefit from work together will very often result in failure or feelings of exploitation."[3] All of these issues can be met if the school library media specialist articulates potential positive outcomes of the proposed collaboration, in order to communicate expectations and help teachers be willing to participate in collaboration. One fact that helps the school media specialist is that most of the people working in schools are truly concerned about helping the children and young adults they work with. This desire to help the students can work in favor of collaboration, once the school library media specialist can show the teachers that collaborating together truly improves instruction and that students benefit from the multitude of skills the two parties bring to the collaboration, and from the resulting enhancement of instruction.

Leader

Collaboration tends to be more successful when one person emerges as the "leader," with a vision and a commitment to the process. This is well stated by Michael C. Roberts in connection with successful collaborative programs for delivering mental health services to children and families: "On the whole, the model programs tend to have been developed and maintained by the enthusiasm of a strong central figure who energizes others in carrying out the program's goals and in maintaining the program's standards."[4] In practice, this means that if a teacher does not function in this capacity, the school library media specialist will need to assume this leadership role.

According to Warren Bennis, four competencies tend to characterize "true leaders." These are:

- Management of attention (has and communicates a vision to others, enticing them to join in the project)
- Management of meaning (has the ability to communicate his or her vision effectively)
- Management of trust (has built a reputation for reliability)

- Management of self (knows self and has confidence in own abilities).[5]

Awareness of these characteristics can help the school library media specialist understand how his or her behavior and communication with others create an atmosphere either supportive of or detrimental to efforts to develop collaboration.

A school library media specialist's taking a leadership role does not necessarily mean the school library media specialist must "take over" administrative patterns of behavior. Lillian Biermann Wehmeyer proposes a quieter, alternative model for school library media specialists: "The *consigliere* is an indirect leader who interacts as a colleague with other faculty members. Such change facilitators do not issue directives; rather, they ask, inform, model, suggest, and support."[6] This model is well suited to the position of the school library media specialist in the school, and it is compatible with the type of collaboration being advocated here.

Based on her work as editor of *Knowledge Quest*, Debbie Abilock has compiled a list of attributes that seem common to collaborative leaders and that are also consistent with the *consigliere* identified by Wehmeyer. The literature of library and information science is the basis for her list. She states that collaborative leaders:

- Envision the ideal and work backward
- Live their core beliefs
- Listen for ideas, then think
- Counter mental models with new knowledge
- Seek to understand
- Ask genuine questions
- Use mediated language
- Treat adults as learners
- Believe in the reliability and credibility of information in books and buy them
- Value thinking together.[7]

There is evidence that this type of interaction in the real world is effective. For example, in the Association for Library Service to Children (ALSC), one committee chair believed wholeheartedly in the value of a training manual for public libraries. Totally committed to this goal, she worked tirelessly to share her vision and convert the rest of the committee to the need for this project. Her belief in the value of the potential publication was so strong that she overcame all obstacles and inertia, without antagonizing other committee members, who were all volunteers. The manual was published, thanks to the commitment of the chair. Without her drive and strong belief, other committee members would have been content to meet a couple of times a year, discuss issues, and wait for the next meeting. The chair's vision galvanized the entire committee. In some schools, the school library media specialist must be the one with the vision for and belief in the benefits of collaboration for the school. Then she or he must convey that belief and that vision to others and work diligently to incorporate collaboration, and information literacy, throughout the school and the curriculum.

It will not necessarily be easy to convince others of the need for and value of collaboration—and it will not be quick. But if the school library media specialist works persistently, reaching one or two teachers a year, it is possible to be successful. If necessary, the school library media specialist *must* take the leadership role in this arena. Keep in mind that as successful collaborations are shared among members of the school community, it will be easier to get more teachers involved.

Reasons for Collaborating with the School Library Media Specialist

It is important for teachers to truly understand why the school library media specialist wants to collaborate with them. For example, in a school with fixed scheduling where students are scheduled for weekly sessions in the school library media center to provide teachers release time for planning, teachers may perceive collaboration as a first step toward flexible scheduling. Under flexible scheduling, the rigid timetable of class visits would change to a system where students come to the school library media center when they need to for class assignments or information-literacy skills. A class may come daily for a week and then not be scheduled again for two weeks. In this type of situation, collaboration may be seen as a threat to teacher planning time, and therefore the teachers may be opposed to collaboration. The school library media specialist must share a vision of the potential value of collaboration involving the school library media specialist with the entire school community, thus contradicting the misperception that collaboration makes the school library media specialist's job easier while increasing the work load for teachers. Again, this will take time, but by working with and converting one teacher at a time, the school library media specialist can eventually convince other professionals of the value of school library media specialist involvement with collaboration.

Common Vocabulary

In addition to clarifying the roles of those involved in collaboration, it is important for all involved to use a common vocabulary. This can be difficult if those collaborating are not aware of varying or contradicting definitions. For example, while writing a book on bibliotherapy, a mental health professional and a school library media professional found that they had differing definitions of the term. Only after discussions about material for the book over a couple of years did the mental health professional finally identify an ongoing reason for communication difficulties. Her definition of bibliotherapy was giving books to clients, who would read them and work to solve their problems in isolation. The school library media specialist, by her definition, would identify an appropriate title for a particular student or group of students, everybody would read it, and then the students and adult professionals would discuss the issues together. Both authors were able to work more smoothly on the book once they had a common definition.

Lack of common vocabulary can hinder discussion; it may even cause enough difficulty to threaten the success of the collaboration. Writing about the need for team members to understand each other's vocabulary, Sidney L. Gardner notes: "What is required is . . . an openness to ask questions, to clarify the differences."[8] So if there seems to be some kind of misunderstanding during discussions, it is prudent to stop and explore possible reasons for the confusion. It may be that the confusion or developing conflict is due to different definitions for ideas, processes, or products under discussion.

Equal Status

True collaboration occurs among people who are respected and equal partners in the process. Marilyn Friend and Lynne Cook state that collaboration requires "a situation in which each person's contribution to an interaction is equally valued and each person has equal power in decision making."[9] Research indicates that one person needs to have the vision, push for collaboration, and initiate contacts and scheduling of meetings. At the same time, during the actual collaboration all participants should be equal. Everyone should feel free to make suggestions, assume responsibility for things they are comfortable with, and express dissenting views. There should not be a "boss" who mandates what will happen, who will do it, and when it will be done, not even an administrator who chooses to become part of the process. Collaboration is a process among partners, in which final decisions are reached by consensus, not by fiat.

As Jehl and Kirst document, "an atmosphere of mutual respect and collegiality, or shared responsibility and control, must pervade."[10] If the collaborative effort is to accomplish anything, it is important for the school library media specialist to be receptive to input from others in the collaboration. It is important for *all* participants to manifest this type of acceptance, but it may also be true that the school library media specialist is the advocate for collaboration or for inclusion in the collaborative process. Therefore, the school library media specialist should model appropriate behavior; with time, all involved should learn acceptance. As Ian M. Evans, Akiko Okifuji, and Allison D. Thomas clearly state, "A true collaboration model assumes mutual respect and recognition."[11]

Preparation

It is important that participants prepare an agenda to help ensure that both the lesson and the perceived roles of all involved are discussed. The school library media specialist should participate in but not dictate formulation of the agenda. If the subject area of the lesson or unit is known in advance, it could be appropriate to bring materials, especially rough drafts of collaboration forms, to the first meeting. The school library media specialist needs to use professional judgment about the people involved to determine exactly what is appropriate. School library media specialists should not convey the attitude that they are in charge; instead, it is important to arrive ready to work with the others. This can be a fine line to walk, but the potential results make it worth the effort.

Successful Teams

In research on collaboration between academic professors in management and practitioners, Teresa M. Amabile and her fellow authors identify three characteristics of successful collaborative teams: "project-relevant skill and knowledge, collaboration skill, and attitudes and motivation."[12]

In a chapter contributed to a book on inclusive education for practicing teachers, Marshall Welch lists key components of collaboration:

- Common goals (participants do indeed share a common goal)
- Interdependence and parity (everybody in the group does an appropriate share of the work needed to accomplish the common goal)
- Interactive exchange of resources (all share information resources, human resources, financial resources, physical resources, and technological resources)
- Decision making (through problem solving and communication, decisions are reached)
- Problem-solving skills (participants are able to identify a problem, generate potential solutions, select a solution, implement that solution, and assess the results)
- Communication skills (in interactions, using "CAPS"—participants *clarify* by seeking additional information when needed, *attend* by listening well, *paraphrase* to ensure understanding, and *summarize* to facilitate further communication).[13]

Summary

- *Identify a common goal—everybody wants to help the students.*
- *Someone needs to provide leadership and the vision for and commitment to collaboration. The school library media specialist may assume this role.*

- *Everybody understands the role of each participant in the collaboration.*
- *The school library media specialist communicates the value of his or her participation in collaboration to all.*
- *Common vocabulary is mandatory.*
- *All participants are equal in status.*
- *School library media specialist is open and receptive to comments from others.*
- *There is an atmosphere of mutual respect.*
- *School library media specialist is prepared for meetings.*

BARRIERS

A school library media specialist beginning to participate in collaboration in the school would be wise to expect some difficulties and some actual barriers. These are common in all types of collaboration among all types of professionals. A variety of things can impede full collaboration between teachers and the school library media specialist.

It is probable that a school library media specialist suggesting his or her personal involvement in collaboration or implementing collaboration in a school will encounter resistance from at least some of the other professionals in the school. There may be a variety of reasons for their resistance. As Barbara Gray notes, "People resist change for several reasons: they do not like the uncertainty associated with change; they feel insecure or afraid of expected consequences of the change; they have an investment in the status quo; or they do not understand or agree with the consequences of the proposed changes."[14]

Within this framework, there may be more specific reasons for resistance to collaboration in the school. Some teachers may fear the idea of collaboration, being convinced that working in the currently established ways is best. Some teachers may just be opposed to change. Some teachers may have heard or read that collaboration is bad and oppose the idea without any personal experience. Some teachers may have had experience with collaboration and found it had little or no value for them. Others may not voice any opposition but also will not actively participate or openly support the idea of collaboration. Some may be comfortable with collaborating with other teachers but see no reason for the school library media specialist to be involved. It is best if the school library media specialist does not react negatively to such attitudes.

Welch classifies barriers to collaboration into four separate categories:

- Conceptual barriers (preconceived expectations of how things are done in *this* school)
- Pragmatic barriers (scheduling, policies, bureaucratic structures)
- Attitudinal barriers (feelings and attitudes about working together)
- Professional barriers (differences in training among professionals).[15]

While not all of these classifications are appropriate, the school library media specialist may use the categories above to understand better some of the resistance encountered during collaboration.

When encountering resistance, the media specialist must decide how to proceed. The first step is to gather information and analyze the situation. As Gray states, "A critical tool for dealing with resistance is understanding what causes it."[16] By talking with and observing those teachers reluctant to participate, the school library media specialist can begin to understand possible causes for the resistance. It is important at this stage to listen with an open mind while gathering information. Results of this data gathering can help the school library media specialist decide what to do next.

Certain individuals may not be willing or able to change. The school library media specialist may be wise to abandon efforts to collaborate with such persons and move on to other individuals. Some people may become more willing to participate when they see the results of successful collaboration with other teachers. Some teachers are willing or even enthusiastic about the idea of collaboration with the school library media specialist. When a teacher or teachers agrees to collaborate with the school library media specialist on a lesson or unit, the school library media specialist must do everything possible to ensure that the collaboration is not only successful but the very best experience possible for the teacher and the students. When word of positive results spreads throughout the school, other teachers may be more willing to collaborate with the school library media specialist. If additional teachers do not contact the media specialist about joint collaborations, the school library media specialist should again reach out and seek teachers willing to collaborate. The same criteria used to solicit teachers to work with can be used again. (This topic was discussed in chapter 3.) With time, those teachers initially opposed can often be won over to the idea of working with the school library media specialist.

In some schools, the administration may require all teachers to collaborate with the library media specialist. In these cases, there will probably be resistance from at least some, if not most, teachers, who may resent what they perceive as interference in their right to teach. If the principal stands firm and finds the needed resources, if the media specialist has the professional training needed, and if both of them work together to do the required planning, the teachers can be converted. While this method is quicker than converting teachers one or two at a time, the administrator and the media specialist need to discuss fully both the ramifications and potential benefits of compulsory collaboration.

In some schools, administrators, teachers, and the school library media specialist may jointly decide to institute mandatory collaboration among all professionals, including the school library media specialist. This is the best of all worlds, and it results in an atmosphere conducive to success for collaboration. Whatever the current system in the school, the school library media specialist must work with it, not fight against it.

When working to overcome either actual or anticipated resistance in a school, the school library media specialist needs to prepare carefully. There are several ways to do this. It is possible to work in advance to identify specific objections likely to be expressed and then articulate responses that disarm those objections. It can be useful, with some personalities, for the school library media specialist to invite individual teachers to develop plans for collaboration in the school. Participation in this kind of activity can build a feeling of ownership among those on the committee. (This can be especially useful if the people involved are perceived to be key people or leaders in the school community.) The school library media specialist could gather data and success stories showing the value of collaboration between teachers and school library media specialists and share them with the school community. A clearly articulated plan showing how and why collaboration can benefit the entire school community may be an important ingredient for some people. A newsletter or website showing ideas the school library media specialist has for this school could also win supporters. Some of this information could be included in an annual "welcome back" packet of materials presented to everybody at the beginning of the school year. Also, as stated above, when a school library media specialist successfully collaborates with some teachers in the school, other teachers may be willing to try collaboration with the school library media specialist too.

Summary

- *Resistance to collaboration may arise from a number of causes.*
- *The school library media specialist can work with individuals to overcome resistance.*
- *Mandatory collaboration has both positive and negative points.*
- *The school library media specialist needs to prepare carefully to respond to objections to collaboration.*

PLANNING FOR SUCCESS

There are undeniably barriers to collaboration among teachers and the school library media specialist, but that does not mean that it is hopeless. As one principal says, "The key to overcoming the barriers is, first of all, to identify them and begin to develop a plan of attack."[17] Specifically, he suggests forming a group of teachers and then asking them what they see as potential barriers to collaboration in the school. This same group can then begin to identify ways to overcome these barriers.

There are other valid approaches to overcoming the barriers, also. Having researched planning and management in the United States and Australia, Richard D. Margerum identifies several reasons for failure of groups to establish collaboration:

- Poor communication
- Problems with resolving conflicts

- Personality differences
- Extremely difficult problems the group needs to solve
- Long histories of antagonism
- Inadequate funding to support implementation.[18]

Examination of this list of potential causes for failure suggests that a proactive school library media specialist could anticipate and plan to avoid these pitfalls when collaborating with teachers.

- Creation and maintenance of appropriate means of communication (e.g., notes, e-mails, newsletters, phone calls) could help the group avoid poor communication. All group members or a single individual could assume responsibility for communication. A common vocabulary helps to avoid communication problems also.
- Some tested, useful methods for dealing with conflict are presented in chapter 5. By becoming familiar with and practicing these and other "people skills," the school library media specialist can model mediation and conflict resolution.
- Personality differences can be a "touchy" area to deal with. If the group is already formed, the school library media specialist can model professional behavior and mutual respect, and try to give input so that the same people are not asked to work together again. If the group is just forming, the best approach is to choose group members carefully to avoid friction, where possible. People who are continually inhibiting collaboration are denying their students access to services and knowledge provided by others. It may be appropriate to bring this issue into the open.
- Careful selection of limited areas for initial collaboration can postpone the more involved curriculum planning issues until the participants are more skilled in collaboration, and therefore better able to deal with difficult or involved issues.
- Where there is a long history of antagonism, everything possible should be done to avoid pushing the antagonists together. This is one reason why it is vital to know and understand the culture of the school before initiating collaboration. Sometimes (albeit rarely), a naïve newcomer is able to overcome this antagonism, but do not count on it.

- Finally, funding is and will continue to be a problem. There is no way, given the structure and funding available in today's schools, that full collaboration can be implemented throughout the school. However, this is not a valid reason for not collaborating. The school library media specialist must either work to join groups already collaborating or initiate collaboration with one or two teachers (or a grade level or a department) and slowly prove the value of collaboration in the school. With time, more support and funding may be made available to enable the school library media specialist to collaborate more often. For example, a school may hire one or more paraprofessionals to free the school library media specialist to plan with teachers; flexible scheduling may be implemented and other arrangements made to provide for teacher prep time. Using the excuse of inadequate funding to avoid collaboration only ensures that it will never happen.

Another way to increase the probability of success in collaboration is to proactively work to establish a procedure to follow that will focus group efforts on the procedure and anticipated outcomes. For example, Welch describes a six-step procedure known as DECIDE. His original six steps are given here, along with connections to collaboration that occur between the school library media specialist and teachers:

- *D*efine the situation. (Identify who, what, where, and when. Situations tend to be very complex, and it may be necessary to also examine the history of the school and the curriculum. Prior experience working with a teacher or teachers may help to decrease the amount of time spent on this step. This is where discussion of individual roles occurs.)
- *E*xamine the environment. (Look at the school curriculum and entire context of the school for connections to the lessons being planned. Identify the place of the lesson being planned in the overall curriculum of the school and/or district.)
- *C*reate a goal statement. (Now, focus on what the lesson or unit should accomplish; while this may seem obvious, it is not unusual for collaborators to have differing understandings about this point.)

- *I*nvent an intervention plan. (This is where the collaboration focuses on developing the lesson plan and activities, assigning responsibility for specific portions of the plan, and all other aspects of instructional design)
- *D*eliver the action plan. (Now it is time to teach the lesson or lessons.)
- *E*valuate the intervention action plan. (This includes the evaluation that occurs during the lesson itself, and an overall evaluation of the entire lesson and the collaborative process after teaching has finished.)[19]

Linda Lachance Wolcott has created another model for planning with teachers.[20] Her strategies are:

- Together, reflect on teaching and learning. (This kind of dialogue during collaboration allows all participants to explore, share, and articulate all aspects of instruction. Wolcott sees this as a technique allowing both teachers and school library media specialists to tap into the rich knowledge both have of their subject, of teaching methods, and of students.)
- Approach the planning process from the teachers' perspective. (The actual planning process followed by teachers may be more random and nonlinear than the models proposed in pedagogical literature. As long as all elements of the lesson are addressed, the pattern followed is not important.)
- Accommodate various types and styles of planning. (The teachers and school library media specialist working together need to apply all collaborative skills and be very accepting and nonjudgmental about the various approaches to planning.)
- Provide the leadership. (As mentioned above, someone must reach out and advocate collaboration within the school.)

Whether one of these or some other model for anticipating and proactively countering barriers to collaboration is appropriate, the school library media specialist must anticipate problems and work with teachers to overcome them before these problems hinder collaboration.

Summary

- *Anticipate and work to counteract those things that could cause collaboration to fail.*
- *Use one or more of the following strategies, if appropriate:*

  - *Work with teachers to identify and plan to overcome barriers before collaboration begins.*
  - *Devise a plan (such as DECIDE) or method to guide collaboration:*

    - *Examine the situation*
    - *Make sure everybody agrees about the outcome being sought*
    - *Carefully plan for and implement the instruction*
    - *Evaluate both the product and the process.*

  - *Follow Wolcott's model for planning with teachers.*

CONCLUSION

Marshall Welch and Beth Tulbert surveyed teachers, special education teachers, administrators, and related service providers, and analyzed the results to identify the significant components of successful collaboration:

- *Flexibility* is defined as the ability to compromise and to accept change and new ideas.
- *Communication skills* are characterized as listening, the ability to express ideas, and using appropriate body language.
- *Problem solving* includes the skills of identifying needs, brainstorming, evaluating, and adjusting the plan of action.
- *Action plan development* includes identifying activities, needs, and steps for addressing the issue or dilemma.
- *Evaluation, monitoring, readjustment, and feedback* are conceptualized as conducting ongoing assessment of the action plan and modifying as needed.[21]

Some professionals may believe that these procedures will work in a utopia, but not in the real world. There is anecdotal testimony and some research evidence, including from the Library Power project, showing that it is possible for school library media specialists to participate in collaboration with teachers in schools.[22] In some cases, the school library media specialist joins teachers already engaged in collaborative planning; in other cases, the school library media specialist initiates collaboration with teachers in the school. In either case, the potential value added to the school by a fully involved school library media specialist is too great for school library media specialists not to collaborate with teachers.

NOTES

1. Howard S. Adelman, "School-Linked Mental Health Interventions: Toward Mechanisms for Service Coordination and Integration," *Journal of Community Psychology* 21 (October 1993), 313.

2. Jeanne Jehl and Michael W. Kirst, "Getting Ready to Provide School-Linked Services: What Schools Must Do," *Education and Urban Society* 25, no. 2 (February 1993), 157.

3. Melvin Delgado, "A Guide for School-Based Personnel Collaborating with Puerto Rican Natural Support Systems," *New Schools, New Communities* 12, no. 3 (Spring 1996), 39.

4. Michael C. Roberts, "Models for Service Delivery in Children's Mental Health: Common Characteristics," *Journal of Clinical Child Psychology* 23 (1994), 217.

5. Warren Bennis, "The Four Competencies of Leadership," *School Library Media Quarterly* 15, no. 4 (Summer 1987), 197–198.

6. Lillian Biermann Wehmeyer, "Indirect Leadership: The Library Media Specialist as *Consigliere*," *School Library Media Quarterly* 15, no. 4 (Summer 1987), 2001.

7. Debbie Abilock, "Ten Attributes of Collaborative Leaders," *Knowledge Quest* 31, no. 2 (November/December 2002), 8–10.

8. Sidney L. Gardner, "Key Issues in Developing School-Linked Integrated Services," *Education and Urban Society* 25, no. 2 (February 1993), 144.

9. Marilyn Friend and Lynne Cook, *Interactions: Collaboration Skills for School Professionals* (New York: Longman, 1992), 7.

10. Jehl and Kirst, "Getting Ready to Provide School-Linked Services," 156.

11. Ian M. Evans, Akiko Okifuji, and Allison D. Thomas, "Home–School Partnerships: Involving Families in the Educational Process," in *Staying in*

School: Partnerships for Educational Change, ed. Ian M. Evans et al. (Baltimore: Paul H. Brookes, 1995), 31.

12. Teresa M. Amabile, Chelley Patterson, Jennifer Meuller, Tom Wojcik, Paul Odomirok, Mel Marsh, and Steven J. Kramer, "Academic–Practitioner Collaboration in Management Research: A Case of Cross-Profession Collaboration," *Academy of Management Journal* 44 (April 2001), 419.

13. Marshall Welch, "Collaboration as a Tool for Inclusion," in *Inclusive Education: A Casebook and Readings for Prospective and Practicing Teachers*, ed. by Suzanne E. Wade (Mahwah, N.J.: L. Erlbaum Associates, 2000), 74–80.

14. Barbara Gray, *Collaborating: Finding Common Ground for Multiparty Problems* (San Francisco: Jossey-Bass, 1989), 247.

15. Welch, "Collaboration as a Tool for Inclusion," 81–84.

16. Gray, *Collaborating*, 247.

17. David Sanders, "A Principal's Perspective," *Knowledge Quest* 31, no. 2 (November/December 2002), 31.

18. Richard D. Margerum, "Getting Past Yes: From Capital Creation to Action," *Journal of Planning Literature* 14, no. 2 (Spring 1999), 184.

19. Marshall Welch, "The DECIDE Strategy for Decision Making and Problem Solving: A Workshop Template for Preparing Professionals for Educational Partnerships," *Journal of Educational and Psychological Consultation* 10, no. 4 (1999), 363–375.

20. Linda Lachance Wolcott, "Understanding How Teachers Plan: Strategies for Successful Instructional Partnerships," *School Library Media Quarterly* 22, no. 3 (Spring 1994), 163–164.

21. Marshall Welch and Beth Tulbert, "Practitioners' Perspectives of Collaboration: A Social Validation and Factor Analysis," *Journal of Educational and Psychological Consultation* 11, nos. 3, 4 (2000), 369.

22. Norman Webb and Carol A. Doll, "Contributions of Library Power to Collaborations between Librarians and Teachers," *School Libraries Worldwide* 5, no. 2 (July 1999), 29–44.

CHAPTER 5

Interpersonal Skills and Collaboration

Throughout collaborative sessions, it is important for all participants to remember and actively use all the interpersonal skills they have acquired through educational, professional, and personal experience. While such skills are important in all human interactions, they are even more important in collaboration where the school library media specialist is trying to participate in interactions with teachers and also to demonstrate how an "all inclusive" form of collaboration can truly enhance instruction. The school library media specialist may also need to assume the leadership role in this respect and model appropriate behavior for others. Also, the school library media specialist, whether joining an established group or instigating collaboration, needs to do everything possible to ensure success. These skills presented in this chapter will help in that effort.

PROFESSIONAL ATTITUDE

All of the individuals involved in collaboration are professionals, whether teachers, administrators, or the school library media specialist. Ideally, all exhibit professional behavior and courtesy. By listening to each other, truly considering the content of other's comments, arriving on time, and staying on topic, they can help collaboration progress well. The people involved do not have to be close friends, or even like each other, in order to work together. However, each person brings expertise to the collaborative effort, and all involved should respect the knowledge and skills of the others. The school library media specialist should be sure to model such professional behavior during collaboration.

Inappropriate behavior does occur in the workplace; it may be manifested as rudeness, shouting, name calling, harassment, and, rarely, physical acts of slamming or breaking items in the room. However, especially when choosing teachers to approach for collaboration, the school library media specialist should be able to avoid such people. If extreme nonprofessional behavior manifests itself during collaboration, the school library media specialist may leave and end the session. No one must submit to such treatment. Sam Horn's *Tongue Fu* gives some very practical advice on how to respond to and control such situations, while not escalating such behavior.[1]

Summary

- *Everybody should behave professionally.*
- *The school library media specialist may need to model good interpersonal skills.*
- *If inappropriate behavior occurs, the school library media specialist and others may leave the session.*

NONVERBAL COMMU. .ICATION

People do not communicate with each other only by word and voice. Nonverbal communication is an equally important part of interactions among people. Nonverbal communication can take a number of forms, all of which have an impact on those around us.

Body language is one example of nonverbal communication. If someone is facing you, leaning forward a little, watching your face, and even extending a hand in your direction, you feel like they are "tuned in" to you. Someone who sits sideways, turning a shoulder or back toward you, leans away, and will not look at you creates the impression he or she is not interested and would rather be elsewhere. Being aware of the body language among the people working together can be very helpful in determining who is involved and who is not. It can also be an indication of potential conflict with, or less than full support from, team members.

Facial expressions, another form of nonverbal communication, can show approval, encouragement, distrust, impatience, and many more feelings. Smiles, frowns, and rolling eyes are among the techniques humans use to communicate. Also, many other body movements can be used to convey meaning. Shrugging shoulders, tapping a finger impatiently, or nodding or shaking the head are among these. The school library media specialist should be aware of all nonverbal communications among the team. Knowledge acquired through observation can be useful in efforts to get the group to work well together.

Summary

- *Body language is an important part of communication.*
- *Facial expressions and body movements also convey feelings and opinions.*

LISTENING

One of the most valuable tools available to collaborators is taking the time to listen to other participants in the collaboration. "Effective listening is one of the most important of all communication skills. Fortunately, it is one that can be learned. This means that it can be analyzed, understood, and improved. Listening skills affect the quality of personal and professional relationships."[2] When listening carefully, an individual is paying attention to what others are saying and how they are saying it. As Marion E. Haynes notes, "This means learning to pay attention not only to the speaker's words but to their context, to note what's not said, to listen with a purpose, to minimize distractions, and to interpret nonverbal behavior and tone of voice."[3] On the basis of what that person says, the listener makes suggestions, builds on ideas shared, or disagrees in a positive way. In order to succeed, the listener must be open to different ideas and viewpoints. This means the school library media specialist does not enter collaboration with a fully realized lesson plan but instead is ready to work jointly with others to create something new. By creating something new, the group builds on and incorporates input from all members—no one person dominates the "good" suggestions. It is a process of give and take and of free-flowing brainstorming. If this is to happen, effective listening should be used by all participants; it can be modeled by the school library media specialist. The techniques suggested for planning with teachers by Linda Lachance Wolcott, and discussed in chapter 4, can help.

While another person is speaking, one should not be daydreaming, concentrating on formulating his or her own reply, or tuning the person out while planning dinner. Depending on the situation and personalities involved, it may be appropriate to take notes, use a memory-jogging technique (such as holding the appropriate number of fingers to remind yourself to make a certain number of points), or give nonverbal clues of encouragement (such as nodding your head).

As the collaborators are interacting, it is important not to interrupt other speakers. This may not always be the rude act of beginning to speak while someone else is still talking, but even includes "crowding" the speaker. An individual may begin talking over the last few words of the current speaker or immediately upon the conclusion of a sentence of another person. Ideally, all participants are courteously listening to each other and allowing a couple of seconds of quiet pause as each person quits speaking. If constant interrupting becomes an issue, the group may need to address the issue and discuss ways to eliminate these behaviors. Sometimes, simply bringing these behaviors to the attention of group members is enough to solve the problem.

Listening well to others is also complicated by the fact that those who are communicating bring a wide variety of backgrounds and life experiences to the process. "Hearing accurately, which includes being aware of unspoken signals, is difficult because people's values, intellect, feelings, needs, motives, and life stances are unique to them and, by definition, different from other people's."[4] This means that the school library media specialist must meet the challenge of becoming an effective listener in order to model it for other collaborators. "Carl Rogers . . . identified three conditions essential to the process of listening: empathy, acceptance, and congruence."[5] Empathy and acceptance are self-evident. Congruence, in this context, means that the school library media specialist shares honest reactions to the suggestions of other collaborators.

As the school library media specialist works to develop and refine listening skills, *Interactions: Collaboration Skills for School Professionals* by Marilyn Friend and Lynne Cook and *Collaboration for Inclusive Education: Developing Successful Programs* by Chriss Walther-Thomas and others give a more detailed treatment of listening skills, as well as references to other sources for further reading.

Summary

- *Pay attention to those speaking, and then respond to the content of their speech, either physically or verbally.*
- *Stay tuned in to others as they talk.*
- *Do not interrupt.*
- *Different life experiences and training can make effective listening a challenge.*

UNDERSTANDING OTHERS

As people work together in teams, it is important to understand and respect the points of view of other members of the team. Everyone needs to remember that all people are different and to respect those differences. As Friend and Cook say, "Your past experiences, acquired attitudes and beliefs, personal qualities, past and present feelings, and expectations for others affect what and how you observe and perceive, and ultimately how you respond and act."[6] This is often identified in the professional literature as "frame of reference."

In interpersonal relations, making the effort to understand someone else's point of view is vital to the success of joint efforts. In school situations, this means that the school library media specialist, the teachers, and the administrators all bring different agendas to the collaboration. Collaboration is not impossible; however, team members should be aware of the differences, respect those differences, and take advantage of them to build stronger instructional events.

Miscommunication during the collaborative process can result in misunderstandings. These misunderstandings can lead to conflict when in reality the people involved are not on opposite or differing sides. Because of individual differences or training, they do not realize that they are both saying the same thing. This type of situation highlights the value of good listening skills. A careful, neutral exploration of what everyone is saying can often clear up the issue, after which collaboration can continue.

Sometimes, people truly do disagree with each other. It is important to realize that this does not automatically mean that one of them is wrong. For example, if a teacher disagrees with the school library media specialist, there are several possibilities:

- The school library media specialist's position could be valid.
- The teacher's position could be valid.
- Positions of both the teacher and the school library media specialist could be valid.
- Neither positions may be valid.

The following section offers several techniques to employ when disagreements occur.

It can be difficult sometimes to stop, step back, and examine all aspects of an issue in an unbiased, calm environment when disagreements arise. But it is important to remember that it is possible for anyone to be wrong and for honest misunderstandings to occur. If team members can remember and act on that reality, collaboration will be easier to establish.

Summary

- *Respect the frame of reference of other team members.*
- *Remember that miscommunication can sometimes cause disagreements.*
- *Realize that your position may or may not be valid in any given situation, and that the same is true for others.*

DISAGREEMENTS

As individuals share and create ideas while planning a lesson or a unit, or an entire curriculum, disagreements will occur. According to

Martha E. Snell and Rachell Janney, "Effective teams don't necessarily avoid conflict; instead, they minimize conflict, recognize it when it occurs, and establish strategies to address it."[7] It is important for team members to realize that they will have disagreements and then to work together to address and deal with the issues that arise. Examining collaboration between researchers and practitioners in management, Teresa Amabile et al. note that "of all the new insights generated by our examination . . . perhaps the most striking was the important role of conflict resolution processes."[8] That is, the literature suggests that collaborative teams must both realize that conflict will inevitably occur and have the skills needed to resolve or defuse it. There can be a number of responses to disagreements; which one is appropriate depends on the situation and the specific issue and individuals involved.

Stand Firm

The school library media specialist or other individuals may choose to stand firm and refuse to adapt to the position of the other person. When this stance is taken, the school library media specialist must realize that it does not enhance the collaborative environment. However, there are rare occasions where it may be appropriate. For example, if a teacher insists that the school library media specialist must copy or show a videotape in violation of copyright law, refusal to do so would be justified. Ideally, it would be possible to explain or support this refusal with an explanation of the law, but people are not always responsive to reason.

Give In

The school library media specialist or other individuals may choose to accept other individuals' stances and "do things their way." This approach may indeed enhance the collaborative environment, and that may be the primary reason for acquiescence. When the issues are truly trivial or vitally important to other individuals, this may be the appropriate reaction. For example, if it truly does not matter whether or not the group meets in the school library media center or a teacher's classroom but one teacher insists that the planning session occur in her classroom, it can be beneficial to meet in the classroom. This type of acquiescence is appropriate only when other important elements of the collaboration, the unit, or the situation are not adversely affected.

Compromise

Another appropriate way to settle disputes is through compromise. In this situation, both sides give up something to reach a final agreement acceptable to all. Compromise does not have to be a "lose–lose" scenario. For example, two teachers may both have valid reasons for wanting to schedule time in the school library media center at 10:00 AM on Wednesday mornings for the next four weeks. Neither teacher has a "more important" reason than the other. It is impossible for both classes to come at the same time. If the two teachers and the school library media specialist can meet and calmly discuss the situation, it might be possible to work out a compromise agreement. For example, the teachers can take turns coming at 10:00 AM and use 2:00 PM as an alternative time for the second class. Compromises can evolve when the individuals involved trust each other, respect varying viewpoints, and can calmly discuss all of the factors involved. Furthermore, they can be "win–win" situations, although no individual gets everything they wanted.

Collaboration

Collaboration is another way to reach decisions and settle issues. In collaboration, all parties listen to each other and propose a variety of ways to resolve their concerns or solve problems. Ideally, this can happen without personal ownership becoming an obstacle. Instead, all involved make a mutual effort to reach a solution. For example, two colleagues may meet to figure out how to involve alumni in interviews for a new faculty member. In the past, the Alumni Association had hosted a reception. While moderately successful, the reception resulted in a lot of work and expense for the association. After the ramifications of the problem were explored, the colleagues recognized they wanted some way for the Alumni Association to be involved in the search process that was not a burden for the group. What emerged was the idea of inviting two Alumni Association members to join each candidate for dinner one night, along with some search committee members. This suggestion was welcomed by the alumni group. Neither colleague knew exactly how the idea evolved; it was an entirely new procedure to both. This joint development of ideas, procedures, or resolutions to problems is a hallmark of collaboration—and this is what collaboration should foster and encourage in the school. The school library media specialist should join or initiate group interactions to model or instigate this process.

Snell and Janney in *Collaborative Teaming*, Friend and Cook in *Interactions: Collaboration Skills for School Professionals*, and Walther-Thomas and others in *Collaboration for Inclusive Education: Developing Successful Programs* all explore this issue in more depth. Snell and Janney are most helpful in presenting suggestions for developing techniques to deal with conflict during collaboration.

O.F.T.E.N.

Sometimes, the school library media specialist or other collaborative team members may use a conflict-resolution procedure to address the contentious issue before collaboration continues. Marshall Welch presents one model, referred to as "O.F.T.E.N." This technique involves following five steps, using the word "often" as a mnemonic device:

- O = Observation (give an objective description of the situation and the issue)
- F = Feelings (articulate your personal feelings)
- T = Thinking (share your nonaccusatory thoughts about what you believe may have caused the situation)
- E = Expectations (everybody shares expectations they have about resolving the conflict and continuing the collaboration)
- N = Negotiation (everybody works to identify ways to meet the expectations expressed during the previous steps).[9]

Ignoring conflict, while it may be tempting, usually means that conflict will continue, and it may even undermine the entire collaborative process. The strategy suggested by Welch gives one approach that may be useful. It is important that the emphasis is on neutral, respectful exploration of the situation and on involving all involved in the effort to resolve any issues identified. At the same time, Welch acknowledges that "the harsh reality [is] that conflict cannot always be resolved, hence the use of the term 'conflict management' rather than 'conflict resolution.'"[10] So, while attempting to deal with conflict, it is important to remember that not all conflicts can be settled.

Mediation

The techniques presented above for dealing with conflict are primarily suggested as ways for group members to identify and solve disagreements within the group itself. In some situations, the collaborators may wish to call in an outside mediator—for instance, another teacher or an administrator—to help them settle disagreements. This does not happen very often, and only in situations where the individuals involved sincerely want or need to continue the collaboration but are themselves unable to resolve the issue. The outside person must be someone everyone trusts and believes to be fair. The collaborators should agree in advance to abide by the decision of the mediator. When the dispute is settled in this way, participants in the collaboration may feel more confident in the neutrality of the final outcome than if the participants themselves reached a decision. The potential does exist, however, for the "loser" to be dissatisfied, in spite of prior agreements to abide by the mediator's decision.

When the collaboration is expected to continue over time, it is important for the group to develop a method to deal with disagreements that are more than trivial. Mark Soler and Carole Shauffer note, "The method of dispute resolution need not be overly formal, but it should include basic elements of due process to guarantee fairness, including . . . an opportunity to be heard by a neutral decision maker, and a record of the decision resolving the dispute."[11] This does not mean that two people beginning to work together should formalize a dispute-settlement procedure before collaboration begins. It does mean that as collaboration becomes more widespread throughout the school community, dispute resolution is an issue that needs to be addressed.

Summary

Disagreements will occur, and there a various means of resolution:

- *Stand firm*
- *Give in*
- *Compromise*
- *Collaborate*
- *Implement the steps of OFTEN*
- *Use a mediator.*

EVOLVING RELATIONSHIPS

As individuals begin to collaborate, they may be new to interacting with each other in this particular type of situation. Also, if people have collaborated before but a new person is added to the group, the new group will need to reestablish relationships. At the beginning, people may be unsure of what will happen. They may not know how others will react to their suggestions or what others can contribute. As with any new situation, participants may not be convinced of the value of collaboration. Some of our interactions with other people are consciously planned, and some of them are subconscious. In any case, awareness of some of the issues in evolving relationships can benefit our understanding of interactions among the people collaborating with each other.

With time, participants will begin to understand each other and understand what each brings to the collaboration. As the group works together, confidence will build—in terms of the contributions each person can make and in terms of the ability of the group to actually create and deliver improved lessons to students. With success, the participants will begin to value collaboration and what it adds to the school community.

Friend and Cook state that those people who are involved in collaboration come to appreciate this style of working. "Typically, success in collaboration leads to increased commitment to future collaboration, and so beliefs and attitudes become increasingly positive."[12]

Summary

- *Initially, collaborators may be unsure of each other and the process.*
- *With time, collaborators begin to value the process.*
- *When new members are added, relationships need to be redefined and evolve again.*

CONCLUSION

In an article describing a course designed to be part of the education curriculum at the University of Utah, Welch and his fellow authors indicate that for effective collaboration, professionals must have the ability to:

- Take the perspective of others
- Speak a common language
- Manage conflict
- Conceptualize school problems in a broad fashion, and
- Share resources, knowledge and skills.[13]

"People skills" and a professional attitude are vitally important to successful collaboration. Initially, the school library media specialist may need to model these skills and attitudes during group meetings. With strong leadership in this area, the proper atmosphere should evolve to foster collaboration. Furthermore, once teachers and the school library media specialist succeed in working together, it is likely they will be more willing to continue collaborating in the future.

NOTES

1. Sam Horn, *Tongue Fu: How to Deflect, Disarm, and Defuse Any Verbal Conflict* (New York: St. Martin's, 1996).

2. Chriss Walther-Thomas, Lori Korinek, Virginia L. McLaughlin, and Brenda Toler Williams, *Collaboration for Inclusive Education: Developing Successful Programs* (Boston: Allyn and Bacon, 2000), 98.

3. Marion E. Haynes, "Becoming an Effective Listener," *Supervisory Management* (August 1979), 21.

4. D. Newton, *Feed Your Eagles! Building and Managing a Top-Flight Sales Force* (Englewood Cliffs, N.J.: 1991), 119.

5. Newton, *Feed Your Eagles!* 119.

6. Marilyn Friend and Lynne Cook, *Interactions: Collaboration Skills for School Professionals* (New York: Longman, 1992), 129.

7. Martha E. Snell and Rachel Janney, *Collaborative Teaming* (Baltimore: Paul H. Brookes, 2000), 32.

8. Teresa M. Amabile, Chelley Patterson, Jennifer Meuller, Tom Wojcik, Paul Odomirok, Mel Marsh, and Steven J. Kramer, "Academic–Practitioner Collaboration in Management Research: A Case of Cross-Profession Collaboration," *Academy of Management Journal* 44, no. 2 (April 2001), 428.

9. Marshall Welch, "The O.F.T.E.N. Strategy for Conflict Management," *Journal of Educational and Psychological Consultation* 12, no. 3 (2001), 258–260.

10. Welch, "The O.F.T.E.N. Strategy for Conflict Management," 260.

11. Mark Soler and Carole Shauffer, "Fighting Fragmentation: Coordination of Services for Children and Families," *Education and Urban Society* 25, no. 2 (February 1993), 137.

12. Friend and Cook, *Interactions*, 10.

13. Marshall Welch, Susan M. Sheridan, Addie Fuhriman, Ann W. Hart, Michael L. Connell, and Trish Stoddart, "Preparing Professionals for Educational Partnerships: An Interdisciplinary Approach," *Journal of Educational and Psychological Consultation* 3, no. 1 (1992), 2.

CHAPTER 6

Information Literacy Models

One important aspect of the school library media specialist's work today is helping to integrate information literacy throughout the school curriculum by collaborating with teachers, teaching students directly, and serving on curriculum committees. In the professional literature for library and information science, there are numerous models suggesting steps to teach students to follow as they learn to search for and use information. Several of those models are discussed below.

For each model, a brief listing of the recommended steps is followed by comments or explanations. Some steps are common to most, if not all, of the models. This selection is not intended to be an exhaustive presentation of all options available, merely a beginning. Use your professional judgment and knowledge of your school, teachers, and students to help you decide which would be most useful in your situation. It is important to consult the state standards or benchmarks for information literacy that apply to your location. Finally, you may find this information helpful when working with teachers either to design curriculum or to plan specific learning activities.

AMERICAN ASSOCIATION OF SCHOOL LIBRARIANS

The American Association of School Librarians (AASL) of the American Library Association (ALA) issued a position paper, "Information

Literacy: A Position Paper on Information Problem Solving," in 1994. This "Information Problem-Solving Skills" model includes these steps:

- Defining the need for information
- Initiating the search strategy
- Locating the resources
- Assessing and comprehending the information
- Interpreting the information
- Communicating the information
- Evaluating the product and process.[1]

Under each of the steps listed above, a brief explanatory statement and three to twelve competencies for student learning are supplied.

This model was developed under the auspices of the national professional organization for school library media specialists. The introductory matter defines information literacy and its role in the school and explores the role of the school library media specialist in information literacy, while scenarios from the Wisconsin Educational Media Association at the end show possible learning experiences based on these seven steps.

BIG SIX

Michael B. Eisenberg and Robert E. Berkowitz created their model for a procedure to be used to seek information, which, as the name of the process implies, has six steps:

- Task definition
- Information-seeking strategies
- Location and access
- Use of information
- Synthesis
- Evaluation.[2]

This is perhaps the best known and most widely used of these models. Innumerable articles, websites, and books suggest a variety of ways to actually use Big Six in schools. Eisenberg and Berkowitz themselves have continued to publish additional information on this model. It is very flexible and can be used with almost any grade. Indeed, the same six steps could be followed by anyone seeking information to make daily decisions.

SUPER THREE

Recently, an early-childhood version of Big Six has been developed. It is called Super Three. Three steps have been defined: Beginning, Middle, and End.[3] This adaptation may allow the basic principles of Big Six to be used with a younger audience. You will need to decide whether or not it is suitable for your students and your curriculum.

EIGHT Ws

Annette Lamb proposes a set of eight steps for an information-seeking model she suggests would enhance project-based learning:

- Watching (observe the environment around you)
- Wondering (explore questions and ideas and thoughts)
- Webbing (begin to find information and link ideas)
- Wiggling (manipulate the information looking for patterns, clues, ideas)
- Weaving (use the information found to create new products)
- Wrapping (solidify the ideas, solutions, new creations from Weaving)
- Waving (share ideas, communicate findings, get feedback)
- Wishing (evaluate the product and the process).[4]

While Lamb's process is most appropriate for younger children, it does stress the value in making a wide variety of information sources available to students. If you would like more information on this model, the website includes may links to sources for both adults and children.

FOLLETT

The Follett Software Company published its Information Skills Model, by Marjorie Pappas and Anne Tepe, in 1995. The basic steps in this version of an information literacy model are:

1. Questions

    • Develop an overview
    • Integrate broad concepts

2. Specific Questions/Identify Thesis/Plan Search Strategy

    • Locate information providers
    • Identify information resources and tools
    • Search for relevant information

3. Assess and Reflect

    • Interpret information

4. Apply Information/Construct New Knowledge

    • Organize and format information
    • Share new knowledge

5. Searcher Evaluation

    • Evaluate both product and process.[5]

Pappas and Tepe created an involved schematic that portrays this complicated process graphically. For some learners, an opportunity to see the entire procedure visually depicted could be very helpful. Also, this model articulates an extremely wide variety of possible actions or sources that could be appropriate for each step. For example, the information providers listed include: community businesses, home computer resources, all government agencies, all types of libraries, the school library media center, classrooms, historical sites, news services, colleges and universities, nature centers, planetariums, museums, and zoos.

I-SEARCH

Originally developed by Ken Macrorie as a writing model for college undergraduates,[6] this technique has been adapted to use with students in both elementary and secondary schools.[7] I-Search is based on work done by Julie Tallman at Stearns High School in Millinocket, Maine. It contains these steps:

1. Students choose the topic they will research.
2. Students answer these questions about their topic:

   - What do I know?
   - What don't I know?
   - What do I want to find out?

3. In using information, the students make double-entry drafts in their journals noting personal reactions while:

   - Handling, controlling, and connecting information to the research question
   - Comparing and contrasting information and information sources

4. Students write a first draft
5. Student work undergoes peer editing
6. Final reports answer:

   - What I want to know
   - Why the topic is important to me
   - Story of my search for information
   - How I have used information found to answer my question.[8]

The I-Search technique is unique in the importance it places on students' actually identifying topics they want to research. Some of these topics can be quite personal, such as trying to choose the type of dog a child should buy or researching a health problem that affects family members. Sometimes the "selection" may be limited to picking from a list of appropriate topics for a unit of study. However, there should be some element of student choice. At the same time, some students need help in making this selection.

If you are interested in pursuing the I-Search, it would be appropriate to return to Macrorie's work and read about this technique as envisioned by its creator. For one thing, students actually involved in an I-Search should be interviewing experts in the field. Macrorie considers this element of networking with real people key to the process.

KUHLTHAU

Carol Kuhlthau, a respected library and information science researcher, was a high school library media specialist before becoming a university professor. Her model for information skills is based on extensive research. Each of her seven steps first identifies the task, then addresses students' thoughts, feelings, actions, and strategies. The seven steps, and corresponding feelings students may experience, are:

- Initiating the assignment (apprehension, uncertainty)
- Deciding on a topic (confusion, anxiety, brief elation, anticipation)
- Exploring information (confusion, uncertainty, doubt, threat)
- Forming a focus (optimism, confidence in ability to finish)
- Collecting information (realization of amount of work to be done, confidence, increased interest)
- Preparing to present (relief, satisfaction, disappointment)
- Assessing the process (accomplishment or disappointment).[9]

Kuhlthau has researched and written extensively about how students can and should do research. While her research can be challenging to read, *Teaching the Library Research Process* is an invaluable and clear tool for implementing the results of her work in a school setting. Suggestions are given to help school library media specialists and teachers identify appropriate types of help or recommended interventions at each stage, based on student feelings as identified through research.

POWER SEARCHING

In 1998, Jamie McKenzie published 10 steps as a strategy for searching digital resources. As they appeared in *From Now On: The Educational Technology Journal*, the 10 steps are:

- Question and draw before you search (make lists or diagrams of relevant concepts, keywords, and questions)
- Use only the best (identify and bookmark the best search engine)
- Learn the syntax (learn how to use your search engine)
- Learn the features (the search engine has tools, such as advanced search, and users should take advantage of them)
- Start big and broad, then narrow cautiously
- Browse before grazing (scan the brief descriptions of your hits first)
- Go to the source (search engines do not identify everything; go directly to specific sites when you can. For instance, a government site may be the best source for information about pending legislation)
- Be discrete, precise (now you are ready to use specific, relevant terms)
- Cull your findings (use Boolean operators NOT and AND NOT)
- Be playful (respect your intuition).[10]

McKenzie's electronic journal, *From Now On*, often includes useful articles and information on all aspects of educational technology. This is the only model that concentrates exclusively on the digital environment—which may be both a strength and a weakness.

CONCLUSION

When the school library media specialist is teaching information literacy to students, it can be helpful to analyze and evaluate recommended models for information seeking. This knowledge becomes the basis for informed decisions about how to design the information-literacy curriculum for a specific school. One model may be selected for a specific school or school district, or elements of several models may be combined. The most important thing is to be consistent, not introducing students to additional models until they have been successful with one.

NOTES

1. American Association of School Librarians, *Information Literacy: A Position Paper on Information Problem Solving* (Chicago: American Association of School Librarians, 1994).

2. Michael B. Eisenberg and Robert E. Berkowitz, *Information Problem Solving: The Big Six Skills Approach to Library and Information Skills Instruction* (Norwood, N.J.: Ablex, 1990).

3. Tami J. Little, "The Super Three," academicwisc.edu/redl/classes/Tami/super3/html (March 3, 2003).

4. Annette Lamb, "Wondering, Wiggling, and Weaving: Integrating Web Resources," eduscapes.com/sessions/wiggle/wiggle/html (February 19, 1999).

5. M. L. Pappas and Ann E. Tepe, "Follett Information Skills Model," in *Teaching Electronic Information Skills* (McHenry, Ill.: Follett Software, 1995).

6. Ken Macrorie, *The I-Search Paper* (rev. ed. of *Searching Writing*) (Portsmouth, N.H.: Heinemann, 1988).

7. Donna Duncan and Laura Lockhart, *I-Search, You Search, We All Learn to Research* (New York: Neal-Schuman, 2000); and Marilyn Z. Joyce and Julie I. Tallman, *Making the Writing and Research Connection with the I-Search Process* (New York: Neal-Schuman, 1997).

8. Julie Tallman, "I-Search: An Inquiry-Based, Student-Centered, Research and Writing Process," *Knowledge Quest* 27, no. 1 (September/October), 20–27.

9. Carol Collier Kuhlthau, *Teaching the Library Research Process*, 2nd ed. (Metuchen, N.J.: Scarecrow, 1994).

10. Jamie McKenzie, "Searching for the Grail? Power Searching with Digital Logic," *From Now On: The Educational Technology Journal* 7, no. 4 (January 1998), fno.org/jan98/searching.html (April 15, 2003).

Information Literacy Literature Review
Janet Watt

WHAT IS INFORMATION LITERACY?

"In this next century, an 'educated' graduate will no longer be defined as one who has absorbed a certain body of factual information, but as one who knows how to find, evaluate, and apply needed information"[1] This clearly describes our increased knowledge about learning and the future needs of learners. It also explains the move to a constructivist view of learning that will be discussed later in this literature review. We are now often overwhelmed by the information that is available to us, including traditional reference sources and the Internet. Our technological advances put information at the fingertips of people wherever they may be. Thus, it becomes even more critical to have a broader view of information literacy.

One of the most frequently encountered definitions of information literacy is that of the American Association of School Librarians (AASL) of the American Library Association (ALA). "To be information literate, a person must be able to recognize when information is needed and have the ability to locate, evaluate and use effectively the needed information."[2] This includes formats such as print, visual, media, computer, network, and basic literacies.[3]

The California Media and Library Educator's Association (CMLEA) defines *information literacy* as the ability to access, evaluate, and use information from a variety of sources.[4] David Loertscher, as quoted in Nancy Pickering Thomas, describes information-literate students as "avid readers, critical thinkers, creative thinkers, interested learners, organized investigators, effective communicators, responsible information users, and skilled users of technological tools."[5] Greg Byerly and Carolyn S. Brodie say information literacy is "an organized process of information-seeking." They go on to say that at the very least, information literacy would include accessing information, evaluating information, and using information. Definitions such as these suggest that information-literate individuals are "capable of finding and accessing relevant information in appropriate formats and quantities, of reviewing alternatives critically, and of using the information selectively to meet the challenges of contemporary life."[6]

The American Association of School Librarians adopted a position paper on information problem solving. Experts in the field have told us that a problem-solving approach is the best way to teach information literacy. "To be prepared for a future characterized by change, students must learn to think rationally and creatively, solve problems, manage and retrieve information, and communicate effectively. By mastering information problem-solving skills students will be ready for an information-based society and a technological workplace."[7]

Eric Plotnick identifies three themes evident from the research in information literacy that have implications for curriculum and instruction. These are:

- Information literacy is a process that needs to be taught as part of a continuous long-term process.
- Information-literacy skills instruction must be integrated with the curriculum and reinforced in real-life applications.
- Information literacy skills are needed for success in the world.[8]

From an economic perspective, the workplace mandates that workers be information-literate and be able to locate and interpret information. National and state standards also stress the importance of information literacy. "An analysis of national content standards documents reveals that they all focus on lifelong learning, the ability to think critically, and on the use of new and existing information for problem solving."[9]

The contemporary emphasis on restructuring in education has resulted in a paradigm shift from a behaviorist view of learning to a constructivist one.[10] According to Plotnick, this means that information-literacy skills are essential as students construct their knowledge and create understanding. Some of the terms Plotnick encountered in the literature were "resource-based learning," "authentic learning," "problem-based learning," and "work-based learning."[11] Resource-based learning requires students to be information-literate with respect to a wide variety of print and nonprint formats.[12] All members of the education community have a shared responsibility to help students become information-literate. Students need open access to a wide variety of resources in the classroom, school library media center, and outside the school. The information-literacy curriculum should be integrated into the curriculum, and school library media specialists should work in collaboration with classroom teachers to ensure student mastery of skills.

DO SCHOOL LIBRARY MEDIA CENTERS IMPACT STUDENT LEARNING?

Research was sparse for many years regarding the impact of the school library media program on the learning of students. In 1994, Keith Curry Lance pointed out that there had been only 40 studies and that the majority of them had been done between 1959 and 1979. This, in part, is what led him to conduct his first major study in Colorado. By 2001, Lance concluded, approximately 75 studies had examined the impact of school library media programs on student learning. Some of the studies suggested that having a school library media program with a school library media specialist made a difference, but they were not specific about what factors contributed to this improvement.[13] Now recent research provides solid evidence that school libraries make a significant difference in student learning.

Three statewide studies—in Alaska, Pennsylvania, and Colorado— showed a strong school library media program was related to higher scores on standardized achievement tests—no matter what grade or school was examined.[14] Colorado has now repeated its earlier study, as have other states, with similar results. The Colorado study found that "for the 4th and 7th grades, student reading scores on the Colorado State Assessment correlated with the quality of the library media programs and the involvement of the library media specialist in instructional and leadership activities."[15] The important factors identified through these studies were as follows:

- Library media staffing per hundred students
- Size of the collection
- Expenditures per student
- Networked computers with access to resources, databases, and the Internet
- Time the library media specialist spent in leadership activities
- Time the library media specialist spent meeting with the principal, serving on committees, helping teachers access and use standards information, and meeting with other library media professionals
- Time spent collaborating with teachers.[16]

The Alaska study identified these elements as important to improved test scores:

- Full-time library media specialists
- Teaching of information literacy
- Collaborative planning between school library media specialists and classroom teachers
- Staff development
- Longer library hours
- A cooperative relationship with the public library
- Access to the Internet
- A collection-development policy.[17]

In Pennsylvania, the important characteristics were a full-time library media specialist and support staff. The Pennsylvania study speculated that an increase in staff increased the amount of time spent teaching information skills to students, collaborating with teachers, providing staff development to teachers, serving on curriculum committees, and managing information technology.[18]

A newer survey was developed by Lance to address some of the issues that had been problematic with the first study.[19] For example, the new survey further detailed what was meant by an "instructional role," since this did not appear to be well defined in the initial study. This survey was distributed in the same states as the original study. Results varied somewhat, except in the important aspects of the school library media program. Excellent predictors of student performance were staffing and the level of development of the school library media program. "Where library media programs are better staffed, better stocked, and better funded, academic achievement tends to be higher."[20] Other essential factors were the use of particular teaching activities, leadership, collaboration, and use of technology. While individual student visits to the library media center correlated with improved test scores, group visits did not.

Lance found the following factors to be critical if the school library media specialist is to be an effective advocate for information literacy:

- Support staff who can free the school library media specialist to participate in important meetings
- Support of the principal
- Networked technology
- Resources (funding).[21]

Lance and Marsha J. Rodney repeated the school library media program study in Oregon, and the results there support the previous findings. School library media programs accounted for 3 to 5 percent of the variation in reading test scores. As in the other studies, test scores rose with the level of staffing (professional and support staff), the size of the collection, and increased budget for materials.[22]

A study in Texas also indicated an increase in reading scores on the state's basic skills test in schools with good school library media programs. The data showed that in schools with school library media specialists, an average of 10 percent more children passed the test. This conclusion was supported after the researchers controlled for socioeconomic factors, which are traditionally the best predictors of student success. Things that made a difference included collaboration between the school library media specialist and classroom teachers and up-to-date collections.[23] This study was similar to the studies Lance conducted in Colorado, Alaska, and Pennsylvania.

The Simmons Study of school libraries conducted a statewide survey in Massachusetts in the spring of 1999. The study concluded that students in schools with school library media programs scored higher on the Massachusetts Comprehensive Assessment System. Positive factors included:

- Greater number of books per pupil
- Instruction programs in library skills (elementary and middle/ junior-high levels)
- A full-time librarian (elementary and high school levels)
- More circulation of books
- Longer hours
- Higher per-pupil library expenditures (elementary and middle/ junior high)
- Support staff in the library
- Alignment with state curriculum standards (elementary).[24]

In the 1990s, the DeWitt-Wallace Reader's Digest Fund provided monies for school library media programs—the National Library Power Initiative. Research to document the effects of this large longitudinal study showed seven factors that seemed to make a difference in schools with a positive effect on student learning. These included:

- Shared vision
- Staff development
- Collaborative planning opportunities
- Support by principals
- Support staff
- Other school reforms
- Advocates in the district/community.[25]

"Where Library Power seems to have had the most significant influence on student learning is in those schools where it has been tied to other reform efforts that were moving the climate in the school to a more constructivist approach to learning, centering on inquiry in the research process."[26]

Overall, the research supporting strong school library media programs presents a powerful mandate to improve school library media programs. At the same time, there is still a need for an involved, professional school library media specialist.

WHAT IS THE ROLE OF THE SCHOOL LIBRARY MEDIA SPECIALIST?

The mission of the school library media program is to "ensure that students and staff are effective users of ideas and information."[27] This position paper from the American Association of School Librarians goes on to state that the effective school library media program is designed to provide resources, personnel, and training to students and staff so students may develop independence in using their information-literacy skills, and to identify elements of the school library media specialist's role in the school.

The role includes:

- Working with classroom teachers in partnership to plan, design, deliver, and evaluate instruction using a variety of resources and information problem-solving skills
- Teaching and consulting during the transition from a textbook-centered to a resource-based program
- Providing leadership, expertise, and advocacy in the use of technology and resources
- Forming partnerships with teachers to empower students to become lifelong learners
- Managing the library media center.

The American Association of School Librarians states there are three distinct roles for the school library media specialist—information specialist, teacher, and instructional consultant. Facilities and resources available in the school library media center need to support these three roles.[28]

Citing several research studies, Mark Kaminsky indicates that an approach to information literacy integrating information skills into classroom instruction is the most effective mode for student learning and transfer of this learning to new contexts.[29] Both cooperative program planning and cooperative teaching between the school library media specialist and classroom teacher are critical if this integration is to occur. Interdisciplinary study, regardless of the topic, demands information across a broad spectrum. The school library media specialist plays a critical role in helping students access this information.[30] *Information Power* calls on school librarians "to replace stand-alone lessons, delivered in a predetermined sequence, with fully integrated information skills instruction, planned in cooperation with classroom teachers and delivered according to flexibly planned schedules."[31]

In school library media programs there has been a "paradigm shift from collection-centered focus to library user-centered focus."[32] In collaborating with teachers, the school library media specialist forms a partnership to help students learn across the curriculum. Ken Haycock discovered that "the best pair of predictors of high circulation of materials in the library media center is high extroversion and a high degree of curriculum involvement by the library media specialist."[33] Even when a good program is present, Gary N. Hartzell stresses that school library media specialists need to become more "visible" by becoming more active and by letting people know they make a difference. He makes several suggestions for ways in which school library media specialists can accomplish this goal.[34] Hartzell observes that in spite of their invisibility, school library media specialists are indeed changing to meet new mandates. This is echoed by Nancy Pickering Thomas, who states, "To meet the challenges created by the 'brave new world' of electronic connectivity and globalization and to push critical thinking and lifelong learning to the forefront of their lists of instructional objectives, school librarians have explicitly abandoned an outmoded reliance on collections, resources, and circulation statistics as measures of value and turned their attention and energies to innovative programming and new approaches to instruction."[35]

School library media specialists need to stay up to date on learning theory and curriculum so they can assume a leadership role in their school and work collaboratively with classroom teachers.[36] Differentiation of instruction to meet the range of student needs obliges the school library media specialist to provide an even broader range of materials. Other issues, such as multicultural education, literature-based reading instruction, and whole-language approaches to teaching, have implications for collection development. This is a good reason for the school library media specialist to be closely involved in the curriculum process. Annease Chaney Jones found in her dissertation that elementary school library media specialists felt they should be involved in curriculum, and that high school library media specialists thought they should be involved in collaborative planning of lessons. The reality, however, was that practitioners said they spent very little time in curriculum development.[37]

Carol A. Kearney notes that leadership is also an essential role of the effective school library media specialist. She defines leadership as "the process whereby an individual has an idea, a goal, or a vision and shares it with others, who make the vision their own and draw others to it while the original leader finds ways to celebrate their success."[38] According to Linda Lachance Wolcott, principals do not view the school library media specialist as consistently involved in curriculum.[39] This may explain why Kearney noted that the principal does not see the school library media specialist as having significant influence in curriculum decisions. She also discovered that in contrast to principals, the school library media specialists do see themselves as information specialists and teachers, but involvement with curriculum and collaborative planning is viewed as a more informal role.[40] Perhaps this perception is related to the apparent fact that teachers and principals have little knowledge of the school library media center itself and how it works.[41]

Being a leader requires certain qualities. Kearney has identified characteristics of an effective school library media specialist:

- Has a positive self-concept
- May be shy/reserved but projects warmth
- Is bright, stable, enthusiastic, experimenting/exploring, trusting
- Is able to be self-sufficient
- Is confident of worth as an individual
- Enjoys people, work, variety/diversity
- Views change as a positive challenge
- Values communication
- Communicates effectively
- Is caring and especially attentive to others
- Is able and willing to clarify communication
- Is relatively self-disclosing
- Is uncomfortable with conflict

- Is confident of ability to deal with difficult situations in a professional manner
- Is neither critical nor domineering
- Has no great need for achievement, power, or economic advantage
- Views self as a leader in curriculum development
- Is willing to take the risk of being a leader.[42]

Overall, the research indicates that the person in the position of school library media specialist holds the key to success of the program. They can either embrace their role and "sell" themselves to others or be viewed in the limited traditional role of librarian. The research already cited about the impact of the school library media center tells us that we need to adopt the newer views to move forward with student achievement.

Kearney makes an interesting point when she speaks of the school library media specialist's accomplishments as being dependent on the accomplishments of others.[43] If the school library media specialists also have their own goals, they are or should be tied to the support of teachers and students. The "bottom line" is student achievement.

HOW DO CHILDREN BEST LEARN INFORMATION SKILLS?

Thomas believes strongly that "the technological innovations that have made it possible to link school libraries to the larger, information-rich world beyond their doors have made school librarians realize that the older instructional models and stand-alone lessons, with their concomitant emphasis on reference tools and finding aids, do not serve the needs of contemporary students. Indeed, research indicates that students taught 'library' skills in these ways do not learn them to a degree sufficient to allow them to apply them in other contexts."[44] The Library Power Study found that in-depth understanding and critical thinking improves student learning in schools where the curriculum emphasized student inquiry.[45]

An integrated approach, where the library-skills instruction is part of the curriculum, is more successful, according to published research.[46] The major curriculum areas of mathematics, science, social studies, and language arts all stress application to real-life situations and provide opportunities to embed information-literacy skills into the curriculum.[47] Ross J. Todd conducted several studies to measure the effectiveness of an integrated approach to teaching library skills at the high school level. He found this type of approach increased learning of both information skills and content area skills. Students had higher test scores, better recall, and more concentration/focus on tasks, and were capable of more reflective thinking.[48] Haycock notes that integration of subject-area learning with information skills requires students to use library resources and push teachers and school library media specialists to collaborate in order to integrate skills.[49]

As students become more proficient in reading over their school years, a print-rich environment, including a good collection and full-time school library media specialists, plays a role in their learning of information skills. Furthermore, Haycock also indicates that the advances in technology require school library media specialists to assume at least some of the burden of technology support for classroom teachers.[50] The many choices of information sources tax the school library media specialist's budget. He/she will need to make choices about how students learn best and what materials they need. This necessitates setting priorities for the limited dollars that are available.

MODELS FOR TEACHING INFORMATION LITERACY

Two models of learning seem relevant to helping school library media specialists provide instruction in information literacy, and James O. Carey discusses both. One model is called the "instructional design" or "instructional development" model (cognitive objectivism). It is based on "the traditional instructional design view that the world has an objective, real structure that does exist regardless of how different individuals may internalize and interpret what they experience."[51] This is the underlying philosophy for developing curriculum in a more traditional way. Under this approach:

- Learning outcomes are stated, usually as goals and objectives.
- The skills are linked together sequentially.

- The learner's needs are analyzed.
- The curriculum-related instructional strategies are matched to the learner's needs.
- The teacher prepares instructional materials based on this information.
- The teacher implements and evaluates the instruction.
- Revisions are made as needed.

The other model is the "constructivist" design. In this view, learning is an active process where learners construct meaning as they interpret and interact with their environments. This implies that reality is in the mind of the learner and not a set body of knowledge, as in objectivism. Some unique issues for instructional design arise from this view, such as knowing what students need and then designing instruction around it, when everything is constructed as they learn. This leads us to a problem-solving approach to information literacy. The teacher's role becomes one of preparing materials, according to a planned process, and facilitating learning. In a sense, the teacher designs a "learning environment" to guide students to their own understandings. Carey advocates a combination of these two models.

Carol Kuhlthau has researched extensively to refine the steps of her information-skills model. She identifies the seven stages of the information search process as initiation, selection, exploration, formulation, collection, presentation, and assessment of the process.[52] In her discussion of the data from the Library Power schools, Kuhlthau discusses how learning was improved in those schools. Kuhlthau found that many librarians over the course of the study changed their perceptions of how students learn best to a more inquiry-based approach. They also came to realize the value of collaboration with teachers.[53]

The professional literature suggests that problem solving should be the basis for forming models to teach information literacy.[54] Unfortunately, in her study of schools in New Zealand, Penny Moore found that no more than 27 percent of respondents used an information problem-solving model some or most of the time in learning activities.[55] One example of a combination model for teaching information literacy would be Kuhlthau's problem-solving process approach.[56] Michael B. Eisenberg and Robert K. Berkowitz's "Big Six" approach is another example of a process to follow until students have internalized the strategies.[57] The ultimate goal is to have students transfer their knowledge to new situations using appropriate strategies. Students need a great deal of guidance to reach this stage, so it must encompass their K–12 education.[58]

Kay Bishop focused on high school gifted students to see what process they used in research. She discerned the following stages:

- Receiving the assignment
- Selecting a topic
- Exploring for a focus
- Forming a focus
- Collecting information
- Preparing to present
- Assessing the product and process.[59]

Bishop compared the results of her observations to Kuhlthau's model. The stages of exploring and forming a focus presented the most difficulty for the students in the study. One would assume that gifted students develop independence, since they learn so quickly and can work at sophisticated, abstract levels. In fact, however, this study showed even gifted students are dependent on the teacher for information and guidance. Also, the students were most likely to use books and videos as they did research. It was suggested that more collaboration between the school library media specialist, classroom teacher, and public librarian might help students become more independent in their quest for information and less reliant on the teacher.

There are other models, and they seem to have many components that are similar. These components are:

- Need for information
- Possible sources of information
- Location of information
- Evaluation and organization of information
- Use of information
- Evaluation of process and product.[60]

Given this common set of steps, it may not matter which of the information-literacy models is used as long as it is used consistently, allowing a common vocabulary and continuity from year to year at all schools within a district.

Another term that emerges in relation to students and information-literacy skills is "resource-based learning." This is described by AASL as "learning which results from use of multiple resources."[61] This requires students to be information-literate. They need to be able to find, interpret, analyze, synthesize, evaluate, communicate, and use appropriate information as they learn. The Michigan Department of Education has addressed resource-based learning as well. "A resource-based program is essential to assure lifelong learners who can solve problems, think rationally and creatively, manage and retrieve information, and communicate effectively."[62] While the literature seems to support the value of resource-based learning, actually implementing it in the schools can be difficult. A recent study in New Zealand found that teachers had high agreement on the definition of resource-based learning, but that only about half of them had clear objectives or outcome measures.[63] Fortunately, Katsuko Hara's dissertation demonstrates that resource-based instruction is effective at the elementary level.[64]

CURRICULUM TO HELP STUDENTS BECOME INFORMATION-LITERATE

Barbara K. Stripling nicely summarizes the work of Judy M. Pitts, who says, "Library programs must be based around learning, not around libraries."[65] We should have a constructivist focus in our teaching. Reading research has for years acknowledged the importance of prior knowledge. We know that students comprehend more when they have prior knowledge on a topic. Stripling points out how important prior knowledge is to understanding and using library skills; this prior knowledge gives students a framework for developing new learning that makes sense.[66] When Pitts studied a group of students, she found that prior knowledge played a large role in student information decisions. Students with limited prior knowledge seemed to have inadequate mental models relating to information, seriously limiting their ability to learn.[67] Stripling also notes that we need to consider both content and process in learning. The focus needs to be on the "journey" as well as the product.[68] Thus, learning is a cycle and not a linear process. Problem solving should be the focus of the curriculum, as noted previously in this review of the literature. This curriculum needs to reflect all current knowledge about how students learn. Curriculum and instruction should be "designed flexibly so that students can be independent learners who can connect their learning to real-world experiences. . . . [The] learning environment must support curiosity, independence, connectedness, high expectations, thinking, reading, and collaboration."[69] The focus needs to be on learning and not teaching.

Actual teaching activities often do not match what we know is best practice. Change is a slow process that takes a great deal of time and energy to institutionalize in a school.[70] In 1998, Carey summarized where we were in practice by using library science literature, monitoring LM-NET (an online discussion group for library media specialists), and collecting observations in three states. He found the major constraints limiting implementation of best practice to be staffing patterns, scheduling, and alternate perceptions of the library media specialist's roles/responsibilities. Additionally, there are external constraints, such as state curriculum expectations and testing.[71] Most testing is more objectivist than constructivist in design. Testing usually drives teaching so that schools will look good to the public, thus it is difficult to convince teachers that they need to move to constructivism in their classrooms. Tests using constructivist strategies help move practice faster in that direction. Carey saw "a constructivist trend regarding children and their learning of information, but not regarding children and their construction of cognitive strategies for problem solving."[72] What seems to be endorsed is the combination approach supported in *Information Power*,[73] the most recent national standards for school library media centers, and integrated into both the Big Six and Kuhlthau's process approach models for information-literacy skills. This indicates that although we have not reached a truly constructivist model of learning, we are moving forward on the continuum.

"To improve instruction, school librarians have replaced stand-alone library lessons with a dynamic curriculum that places information skills instruction within the larger frameworks of information seeking and problem solving. Scope and sequence activities, which were anchored to location and access skills, have been superseded by activities that emphasize evaluation of informational resources and information use."[74] It is evident that library instruction does make a difference. The skills taught for current needs include more than merely locating and accessing sources.[75] Donna P. Miller and J'Lynn Anderson;[76] Silvana Carletti, Suzanne Girard, and Kathlene Willing;[77] and Ray Doiron and Judy Davies[78] have all written books that offer many examples of units of study based on an integrated and collaborative approach to teaching information literacy skills.

The American Association of School Librarians has identified the basic steps needed in an information-literacy program. These include:

- Defining the need for information
- Initiating the search strategy
- Locating the resources
- Assessing and comprehending the information
- Interpreting the information
- Communicating the information
- Evaluating the product and process.[79]

The Ontario School Library Association has developed a document with a rationale and model for teaching information literacy. A cross-curricular and interdisciplinary curriculum is advocated in this model. It stresses:

- Information problem-solving as well as specific information-handling skills
- Critical thinking
- Information-based decision making
- Collaboration between parents, teachers, and library media specialists
- A goal of student independence in solving information problems
- Socially responsible attitudes about acquiring, using, and communicating information.[80]

Strands in the Ontario curriculum include research and information problem solving, information technologies, and information and society. "The program in all grades and subject areas is designed to develop information problem solving skills, which include accessing, analyzing, applying, creating and communicating information."[81] Four metaskills guide the strands: reasoning, organizing, communicating, and applying. Feedback from library media specialists in Ontario suggests that the curriculum needs to be consistent, with all grade levels and subjects using the same information problem-solving model.

Ontario uses four stages of research and problem solving, which are:

- Preparing for research, which includes defining information needs, identifying ways to organize information, exploring information, and relating prior knowledge.
- Accessing resources, which includes locating a variety of appropriate resources, selecting information, organizing information, and sharing findings/ideas.
- Processing information, which includes analyzing/evaluating information, testing ideas, sorting information, and synthesizing findings/drawing conclusions.
- Presenting findings and solutions, which includes revising, communicating results, reflecting/evaluating research product and process, and transferring new information to solve problems and make decisions.[82]

CONCLUSION

There is a rich body of research, philosophy, and proposed models for and about information literacy in the professional literature. As school library media specialists work to develop and implement an information-literacy curriculum, they should be guided by what the literature reports and also by their own knowledge of the needs of their school and their students.

NOTES

1. P. S. Breivik and J. A. Senn, *Information Literacy: Educating Children for the 21st Century*, 2nd ed. (Washington, D.C.: National Education Association, 1998): 2.

2. American Association of School Librarians and Association for Educational Communications and Technology, *Information Power: Building Partnerships for Learning* (Chicago: American Library Association, 1998): 1.

3. Eric Plotnick, "Information Literacy," *ERIC Digest*, Syracuse, N.Y.: ERIC Clearinghouse on Information and Technology (1999-02-00), ED 427777, www.ericfacility.net/ericdigests/ed427777.html (accessed September 9, 2004).

4. Nancy Pickering Thomas, *Information Literacy and Information Skills Instruction: Applying Research to Practice in the School Library Media Center* (Englewood, Colo.: Libraries Unlimited, 1999).

5. Thomas, *Information Literacy and Information Skills Instruction,* xviii.

6. Thomas, *Information Literacy and Information Skills Instruction,* xviii.

7. American Association of School Librarians, "A Position Paper on Information Problem Solving" (Chicago: 1994): 1.

8. Plotnick, "Information Literacy."

9. Plotnick, "Information Literacy."

10. Janet Watt Nuckles, "From Behaviorism to Constructivism: An Exploration of Teacher Paradigm Shifts" (dissertation at University of Minnesota, 1993).

11. Plotnick, "Information Literacy."

12. American Association of School Librarians, "A Position Paper on Information Problem Solving" (1994).

13. Keith Curry Lance, "Proof of the Power: Quality Library Media Programs Affect Academic Achievement," *Multimedia Schools* (2001), available at proquest.umi.com; and Keith Curry Lance, "Impact of School Library Media Programs on Academic Achievement," *Teacher Librarian* 29, no. 3 (2002): 29–34.

14. Lance, "Proof of the Power: Quality Library Media Programs Affect Academic Achievement," *Multimedia Schools* (2001), available at proquest.umi.com; Keith Curry Lance, "Impact of School Library Media Programs on Academic Achievement"; and Christine Hamilton-Pennell, Keith Curry Lance, Marcia J. Rodney, and Eugene Hainer, "Dick and Jane Go to the Head of the Class," *School Library Journal* 46, no. 4 (April 2000): 44–47.

15. Hamilton-Pennell et al., "Dick and Jane Go to the Head of the Class," 46.

16. Lance, "Proof of the Power"; Lance, "Impact of School Library Media Programs on Academic Achievement"; and Hamilton-Pennell et al., "Dick and Jane Go to the Head of the Class."

17. Lance, "Proof of the Power"; Lance, "Impact of School Library Media Programs on Academic Achievement"; and Hamilton-Pennell et al., "Dick and Jane Go to the Head of the Class."

18. Hamilton-Pennell et al., "Dick and Jane Go to the Head of the Class."

19. Lance, "Proof of the Power"; and Lance, "Impact of School Library Media Programs on Academic Achievement."

20. Lance, "Impact of School Library Media Programs on Academic Achievement."

21. Lance, "Proof of the Power"; and Lance, "Impact of School Library Media Programs on Academic Achievement."

22. Keith Curry Lance and Marcia J. Rodney, "Teaching Information Literacy Is the Key to Academic Achievement: The Success Story of Oregon School Library Media Programs," *OLA Quarterly* 7, no. 2 (2001): 21–22.

23. EGS Research & Consulting, *Texas School Libraries: Standards, Resources, Services, and Students' Performance*, report prepared for the Texas State Library and Archives Commission (2001); and Andrea Glick, "Texas Study Links Libraries, Test Scores," *School Library Journal* 47, no. 9 (September 2001): 19.

24. James C. Baughman, "School Libraries and MCAS Scores," a paper read at a symposium sponsored by the Graduate School of Library and Information Science, Simmons College, Boston, 2000.

25. Dianne M. Hopkins and Douglas L. Zweizig, "Power to the Media Center (and to the People, Too)," *School Library Journal* 45, no. 5 (May 1999): 25–27.

26. Carol Collier Kuhlthau, "Student Learning in the Library: What Library Power Librarians Say," *School Libraries Worldwide* 5, no. 2 (July 1999): 80.

27. American Association of School Librarians, "A Position Paper on Information Problem Solving" (1994).

28. American Association of School Librarians, "Position Statement on the Value of Library Media Programs in Education, (Chicago: 2000), available at www.ala.org/aasl/positions.

29. Mark Kaminsky, "The Importance of Information Studies," *School Libraries in Canada* 19, no. 2 (1999): 18–22.

30. American Association of School Librarians, "The Role of the School Library Media Program" (1990), www.ala.org/aasl/positions; Gary N. Hartzell, "The Implications of Selected School Reform Approaches for School Library Media Services," *School Library Media Research* 4 (2000), www.ala .org/aasl/SLMR/vol4/reform_main.html; and Doug Johnson, "Whose Goals Are They, Anyway?" *Book Report* 20, no. 1 (2001): 88.

31. American Association of School Librarians and Association for Educational Communications and Technology, *Information Power*, 17.

32. Thomas, *Information Literacy and Information Skills Instruction*, xii.

33. Ken Haycock, "Research in Teacher-Librarianship and Institutionalization of Change," *School Library Media Quarterly* 41, no. 4 (Summer 1995): 227–233

34. Gary N. Hartzell, "The Invisible School Librarian," *School Library Journal* 43, no. 11 (November 1997): 24–29.

35. Thomas, *Information Literacy and Information Skills Instruction,* xi.

36. Hartzell, "The Implications of Selected School Reform Approaches for School Library Media Services."

37. Annease Chaney Jones, "An Analysis of the Theoretical and Actual Curriculum Development Involvement of Georgia School Library Media Specialists" (dissertation at Georgia State University, 1997).

38. Carol A. Kearney, *Curriculum Partner: Redefining the Role of the Library Media Specialist* (Westport, Conn.: Greenwood, 2000): 2.

39. Linda Lachance Wolcott, "Understanding How Teachers Plan: Strategies for Successful Instructional Partnerships," *School Library Media Quarterly* 22, no. 3 (Spring 1994): 161–65.

40. Kearney, *Curriculum Partner.*

41. Gary N. Hartzell, *Building Influence for the School Librarian* (Worthington, Ohio: Linworth, 1994).

42. Kearney, *Curriculum Partner,* 5–6.

43. Kearney, *Curriculum Partner.*

44. Thomas, *Information Literacy and Information Skills Instruction,* xi.

45. Hopkins and Zweizig, "Power to the Media Center (and to the People, Too)."

46. Michael B. Eisenberg and Michael K. Brown, "Current Themes Regarding Library and Information Skills Instruction: Research Supporting and Research Lacking," *School Library Media Quarterly* 20, no. 2 (Winter 1992); Michigan Department of Education, "Information Processing Skills Position Paper," Lansing, MI: Michigan State Board of Education (1992); American Association of School Librarians, "A Position Paper on Information Problem Solving" (1994); Ken Haycock, "What All Librarians Can Learn from Teacher-Librarians: Information Literacy a Key Connector for Libraries," keynote address at the National Information Literacy Conference, University of South Australia-Underdale, 1999; Ross J. Todd, "Integrated Information Skills Instruction: Does It Make a Difference?" *School Library Media Quarterly* 23, no. 2 (Winter 1995): 133–39; Hartzell, "The Implications of Selected School Reform Approaches for School Library Media Services"; and Kearney, *Curriculum Partner.*

47. American Association of School Librarians, "A Position Paper on Information Problem Solving" (1994); and Hartzell, "The Implications of Selected School Reform Approaches for School Library Media Services."

48. Todd, "Integrated Information Skills Instruction."

49. Haycock, "What All Librarians Can Learn from Teacher-Librarians."

50. Haycock, "What All Librarians Can Learn from Teacher-Librarians."

51. James O. Carey, "Library Skills, Information Skills, and Information Literacy: Implications for Teaching and Learning," *School Library MediaResearch* (SLMQ Online) v. 1 (1998), available www.ala.org/aasl/SLMQ.

52. Carol Kuhlthau, *Teaching the Library Research Process*, 2nd ed. (Metuchen, N.J.: Scarecrow, 1994).

53. Kuhlthau, "Student Learning in the Library."

54. Eisenberg and Brown, "Current Themes Regarding Library and Information Skills Instruction: Research Supporting and Research Lacking."

55. Penny Moore, "Primary School Children's Interaction with Library Media," *Teacher Librarian* 27, no. 3 (2000): 7–11.

56. Carol C. Kuhlthau, "Implementing a Process Approach to Information Skills: A Study Identifying Indicators of Success in Library Media Programs," *School Library Media Quarterly* 22, no. 1 (Fall 1993).

57. Michael B. Eisenberg and Robert E. Berkowitz, *Information Problem Solving: The Big Six Skills Approach to Library and Information Skills Instruction* (Norwood, N.J.: Ablex, 1990).

58. Joy McGregor, "Teaching the Research Process: Helping Students Become Lifelong Learners," *NASSP Bulletin* 83, no. 605 (1999): 27–34.

59. Kay Bishop, "Authentic Learning and the Research Processes of Gifted Students," *Gifted Child Quarterly* 44, no. 1 (2000): 54–64.

60. Greg Byerly and Carolyn S. Brodie, "Information Literacy Skills Models: Defining the Choices," in *Learning and Libraries in an Information Age: Principles and Practice,* ed. Barbara K. Stripling (Englewood, Colo.: Libraries Unlimited, 1999).

61. American Association of School Librarians, "A Position Paper on Information Problem Solving" (1994).

62. Michigan Department of Education, "Information Processing Skills Position Paper."

63. Moore, "Primary School Children's Interaction with Library Media."

64. Katsuko Hara, "A Study of Information Skills Instruction in Elementary School: Effectiveness and Teachers' Attitudes" (dissertation at University of Toronto, 1996).

65. Barbara K. Stripling, "Designing Library Media Programs for Student Learning," in *Learning and Libraries in an Information Age: Principles and Practice,* ed. Stripling (Englewood, Colo.: Libraries Unlimited, 1999.

66. Stripling, "Designing Library Media Programs for Student Learning."

67. Judy M. Pitts, "Mental Models of Information: The 1993–94 AASL/ Highsmith Research Award Study," *School Library Media Quarterly* 23 no. 3 (Spring 1995): 177–84.

68. Stripling, "Designing Library Media Programs for Student Learning."

69. Stripling, "Designing Library Media Programs for Student Learning."

70. Sandra Hughes-Hassell, "Implementing Change: What School Library Media Specialists Should Know," *Knowledge Quest* 29, no. 3 (January/February 2001): 11–15; Carrie A. Lowe, "The Role of the School Library Media Specialist in the 21st Century," *ERIC Digest*, Syracuse, N.Y.: ERIC Clearinghouse on Information and Technology (2000-11-00) ED 446 769, www.ericfacility.net/ databases/ERIC_Digests/ed446769.html (accessed September 9, 2004); and Nuckles, "From Behaviorism to Constructivism."

71. Carey, "Library Skills, Information Skills, and Information Literacy."

72. Carey, "Library Skills, Information Skills, and Information Literacy."

73. American Association of School Librarians and Association for Educational Communications and Technology, *Information Power.*

74. Thomas, *Information Literacy and Information Skills Instruction,* xii.

75. Eisenberg and Brown, "Current Themes Regarding Library and Information Skills Instruction."

76. Donna P. Miller and J'Lynn Anderson, *Developing an Integrated Library Program* (Worthington, Ohio: Linworth, 1996).

77. Silvana Carletti, Suzanne Girard, and Kathlene Willing, *The Library/ Classroom Connection* (Portsmouth, N.H.: Heinemann Educational Books, 1991).

78. Ray Doiron and Judy Davies, *Partners in Learning: Students, Teachers, and the School Library* (Englewood, Colo.: Libraries Unlimited, 1998).

79. American Association of School Librarians, "A Position Paper on Information Problem Solving" (1994).

80. Mark Kaminsky, "The Importance of Information Studies," *School Libraries in Canada* 19, no. 2 (1999): 18–22.

81. Kaminsky, "The Importance of Information Studies."

82. Kaminsky, "The Importance of Information Studies."

Bibliography

Abilock, Debbie. "Ten Attributes of Collaborative Leaders." *Knowledge Quest* 31, no. 2 (November/December 2002): 8–10.

Adelman, Howard S. "School-Linked Mental Health Interventions: Toward Mechanisms for Service Coordination and Integration." *Journal of Community Psychology* 21 (October 1993): 309–19.

Amabile, Teresa M., Chelley Patterson, Jennifer Meuller, Tom Wojcik, Paul Odomirok, Mel Marsh, and Steven J. Kramer. "Academic-Practitioner Collaboration in Management Research: A Case of Cross-Profession Collaboration." *Academy of Management Journal* 44 (April 2001): 418–31.

American Association of School Librarians. "Information Literacy: A Position Paper on Information Problem Solving." Chicago: American Association of School Librarians, n.d. Also published in: *Emergency Librarian* 23, no. 2 (November/December 1995): 20–23.

American Association of School Librarians and Association for Educational Communications and Technology. *Information Power: Building Partnerships for Learning*. Chicago: American Library Association, 1998.

Auditore, Peter J. "The Many Faces of Collaboration." Special Supplement to *KMWorld* (March 2003): S4–S5.

Bell, Michael, and Herman L. Totten. "Cooperation in Instruction between Classroom Teachers and School Library Media Specialists." *School Library Media Quarterly* 20, no. 2 (Winter 1992): 79–85.

Bennis, Warren. "The Four Competencies of Leadership." *School Library Media Quarterly* 15, no. 4 (Summer 1987): 197–98.

Bleakley, Ann, and Jackie L. Carrigan. *Resource-Based Learning Activities: Information Literacy for High School Students.* Chicago: American Library Association, 1994.

Bredo, Eric. "Collaborative Relations among Elementary School Teachers." *Sociology of Education* 50, no. 4 (October 1977): 300–9.

Conoley, Jane Close, and Collie W. Conoley. *School Consultation: Practice and Training.* 2nd ed. Boston: Allyn and Bacon, 1992.

Corey, Linda. "The Role of the Library Media Specialist in Standards-Based Learning." *Knowledge Quest* 31, no. 2 (November/December 2002): 21–23.

Cramer, Sharon F. *Collaboration: A Success Strategy for Special Educators.* Boston: Allyn and Bacon, 1998.

Crowson, Robert L., and William Lowe Boyd. "Coordinated Services for Children: Designing Arks for Storms and Seas Unknown." *American Journal of Education* 101, no. 2 (February 1993): 140–79.

Delgado, Melvin. "A Guide for School-Based Personnel Collaborating with Puerto Rican Natural Support Systems." *New Schools, New Communities* 12, no. 3 (Spring 1996): 38–42.

Doktor, Judy E., and John Poertner. "Kentucky's Family Resource Centers: A Community-Based, School-Linked Services Model." *Remedial and Special Education* 17, no. 5 (September 1996): 293–302.

Doll, Beth, et al. "Cohesion and Dissension in a Multi-Agency Family Service Team: A Qualitative Examination of Service Integration." *Children's Services: Social Policy, Research, and Practice* 3, no. 1 (2000): 1–21.

Duncan, Donna, and Laura Lockhart. *I-Search, You Search, We All Learn to Research.* New York: Neal-Schuman, 2000.

Eisenberg, Michael B., and Robert E. Berkowitz. *Information Problem Solving: The Big Six Skills Approach to Library and Information Skills Instruction.* Norwood, N.J.: Ablex, 1990.

Evans, Ian M., Akiko Okifuji, and Allison D. Thomas. "Home–School Partnerships: Involving Families in the Educational Process." In *Staying in School: Partnerships for Educational Change.* Edited by Ian M. Evans, et al. Baltimore: Paul H. Brookes, 1995: 32–40.

Farwell, Sybil. "Successful Models for Collaborative Planning." *Knowledge Quest* 26, no. 2 (January/February 1998): 24–30.

Friend, Marilyn, and Lynne Cook. *Interactions: Collaboration Skills for School Professionals.* New York: Longman, 1992.

Gardner, Sidney L. "Key Issues in Developing School-Linked Integrated Services." *Education and Urban Society* 25, no. 2 (February 1993): 141–52.

Glotzbach, Philip A. "Conditions of Collaboration: A Dean's List of Dos and Don'ts." *Academe* 87, no. 3 (May–June 2001): 16–21.

Gray, Barbara. *Collaborating: Finding Common Ground for Multiparty Problems.* San Francisco: Jossey-Bass, 1989.

Harada, Violet H. "Taking the Lead in Developing Learning Communities." *Knowledge Quest* 31, no. 2 (November/December 2002): 12–16.

Hartzell, Gary N. "The Invisible School Librarian." *Knowledge Quest* 31, no. 2 (November/December 2002): 24–29.

Haynes, Marion E. "Becoming an Effective Listener." *Supervisory Management* (August 1979): 21.

Horn, Sam. *Tongue Fu: How to Deflect, Disarm, and Defuse Any Verbal Conflict.* New York: St. Martin's, 1996.

Jehl, Jeanne, and Michael W. Kirst. "Getting Ready to Provide School-Linked Services: What Schools Must Do." *Education and Urban Society* 25, no. 2 (February 1993): 153–65.

Joyce, Marilyn Z., and Julie I. Tallman. *Making the Writing and Research Connection with the I-Search Process.* New York: Neal-Schuman, 1997.

Kuhlthau, Carol C. "The Process of Learning from Information." *School Libraries Worldwide* 1, no. 1 (1995): 1–12.

——. *Teaching the Library Research Process*, 2nd ed. Metuchen, N.J.: Scarecrow, 1994.

Lamb, Annette. "Wondering, Wiggling, and Weaving: Integrating Web Resources." eduscapes.com/sessions/wiggle/wiggle/html (February 19, 1999).

Lance Keith Curry. "What Research Tells Us about the Importance of School Libraries." (Paper included in the proceedings of the White House Conference on School Libraries, Tuesday, June 4, 2002): 17–22.

Lau, Debra. "What Does Your Boss Think about You?" *School Library Journal* 48, no. 9 (September 2002): 52–55.

Leonard, Lawrence and Pauline Leonard. "The Continuing Trouble with Collaboration: Teachers Talk." *Current Issues in Education* 6, no. 15 (2003): 10 or 14. cie.ed.asu.edu/volume6/number15/ (Accessed February 9, 2004).

Little, Tami J. "The Super 3." academicwisc.edu/redl/classes/Tami/super3/html (March 3, 2003).

Lovse, Denise. "Leadership through Collaboration." *Media Spectrum* 28, no. 2 (Spring 2001): 24–27.

Macrorie, Ken. *The I-Search Paper: Revised Edition of Searching Writing.* Portsmouth, N.H.: Heinemann, 1988.

McKenzie, Jamie. "Searching for the Grail? Power Searching with Digital Logic." *From Now On: The Educational Technology Journal* 7, no. 4 (January 1998). fno.org/jan98/searching.html (April 15, 2003).

Margerum, Richard D. "Getting Past Yes: From Capital Creation to Action." *Journal of Planning Literature* 14 (Spring 1999): 181–92.

Moore, Andy. "Is there a Doctrinaire in the House?" Special Supplement to *KMWorld* (March 2003): S2–S3.

Pappas, M. L., and Ann E. Tepe. "Follet Information Skills Model." In *Teaching Electronic Information Skills*. McHenry, Ill.: Follett Software, 1995: 1–6.

Roberts, Michael C. "Models for Service Delivery in Children's Mental Health: Common Characteristics." *Journal of Clinical Child Psychology* 23 (1994): 212–19.

Robins, Kikanza Nuri, and Raymond D. Terrell. "Women, Power, and the 'Old Boys Club': Ascending to Leadership in Male-Dominated Organizations." *School Library Media Quarterly* 15, no. 4 (Summer 1987): 205–10.

Sanders, David. "A Principal's Perspective." *Knowledge Quest* 31, no. 2 (November/December 2002): 31–32.

Senator, Rochelle B. *Collaboration for Literacy: Creating an Integrated Language Arts Program for Middle Schools*. Westport, Conn.: Greenwood, 1995.

Shannon, Donna M. "Tracking the Transition to a Flexible Access Library Program in Two Library Power Elementary Schools." *School Library Media Quarterly* 24, no. 3 (Spring 1996): 155–63.

Snell, Martha E., and Rachel Janney. *Collaborative Teaming*. Baltimore: Paul H. Brookes, 2000.

Soler, Mark, and Carole Shauffer. "Fighting Fragmentation: Coordination of Services for Children and Families." *Education and Urban Society* 25, no. 2 (February 1993): 129–40.

Students in the Educational Media Masters Program, University of Central Florida. "An Overview of *Information Power: Building Partnerships for Learning*." *Knowledge Quest* 27, no. 3 (January/February 1999): 14–16.

Tallman, Julie. "I-Search: An Inquiry-Based, Student-Centered, Research and Writing Process." *Knowledge Quest* 27, no. 1 (September/October 1998): 20–27.

Tierney, William G. "Why Committees Don't Work: Creating a Structure for Change." *Academe* 87, no. 3 (May–June 2001): 25–29.

van Deusen, Jean Donham. "An Analysis of the Time Use of Elementary School Library Media Specialists and Factors that Influence It." *School Library Media Quarterly* 24, no. 2 (Winter 1996): 85–92.

Walther-Thomas, Chriss, Lori Korinek, Virginia L. McLaughlin, and Brenda Toler Williams. *Collaboration for Inclusive Education: Developing Successful Programs*. Boston: Allyn and Bacon, 2000.

Webb, Norman, and Carol A. Doll. "Contributions of Library Power to Collaborations between Librarians and Teachers." *School Libraries Worldwide* 5, no. 2 (July 1999): 29–44.

Wehmeyer, Lillian Biermann. "Indirect Leadership: The Library Media Specialist as Consigliere." *School Library Media Quarterly* 15, no. 4 (Summer 1987): 200–204.

Weisman, Shirley. "Wisdom from *Windows*." *Knowledge Quest* 31, no. 2 (November/December 2002): 32–33.

Welch, Marshall. "Collaboration as a Tool for Inclusion." In *Inclusive Education: A Casebook and Readings for Prospective and Practicing Teachers.* Edited by Suzanne E. Wade. Mahwah, N.J.: L. Erlbaum Associates, 2000: 71–96.

———. "The DECIDE Strategy for Decision Making and Problem Solving: A Workshop Template for Preparing Professionals for Educational Partnerships." *Journal of Educational and Psychological Consultation* 10, no. 4 (1999): 363–75.

———. "The O.F.T.E.N. Strategy for Conflict Management." *Journal of Educational and Psychological Consultation* 12, no. 3 (2001): 257–62.

Welch, Marshall, and Beth Tulbert. "Practitioners' Perspectives of Collaboration: A Social Validation and Factor Analysis." *Journal of Educational and Psychological Consultation* 11 (3 and 4): 357–78.

Welch, Marshall, Susan M. Sheridan, Addie Fuhriman, Ann W. Hart, Michael L. Connell, and Trish Stoddart. "Preparing Professionals for Educational Partnerships: An Interdisciplinary Approach." *Journal of Educational and Psychological Consultation* 3, no. 1 (1992): 1–23.

Wolcott, Linda Lachance. "Understanding How Teachers Plan: Strategies for Successful Instructional Partnerships." *School Library Media Quarterly* 22, no. 3 (Spring 1994): 161–64.

Index

Abilock, Debbie, 47
administrators, school. *See* school
  administrators
American Association of Schools
  Librarians (AASL): model for
  teaching information literacy,
  100. *See also Information Power:
  Building Partnerships for
  Learning* (AASL/AECT, 1998);
  *Information Power: Guidelines
  for School Library Media
  Programs* (AASL/AECT, 1988)
American Library Association
  (ALA). *See* American Association
  of Schools Librarians (AASL)
Association for Educational
  Computing and Technology
  (AECT). *See Information Power:
  Building Partnerships for
  Learning* (AASL/AECT, 1998);
  *Information Power: Guidelines
  for School Library Media
  Programs* (AASL/AECT, 1988)

Bennis, Warren, 46–47
Big Six information literacy teaching
  model, description, 78

collaboration: barriers to, 51–53;
  compulsive, 19, 54; defined, 3–4;
  failure to collaborate, reasons for,
  56; incentives for, 45–51, 52; and
  interpersonal skills, 63–74;
  mandated by school
  administration, factors influencing
  outcomes, 19; planning strategies,
  57–58; process for, 6; resistance
  to, 22–26, 53–59; resources,
  sharing of, 25; roles, clarification
  of, 49; school administrator
  indifference, overcoming, 15–16;
  skills, 45–60; vital factors for, 24
collaboration, enabling the concept
  of: equality among team
  members, 50; identifying reasons
  for collaboration with school
  library media specialists, 48–49;
  leader, identification of, 46–48;
  vocabulary, common, 49–50
collaboration, planning for:
  evaluation of lesson, 42; first
  meetings with teachers, 36–40,
  41; teaching the lesson, 40–41, 42
collaboration, planning of: initial
  planning stages, 31–34, 34–36;

113

About the Author

Carol A. Doll is professor and associate dean in the School of Information Science and Policy at the University at Albany, where she teaches courses on youth services in both public libraries and school library media centers. She has taught in library and information science education since earning her doctorate at the University of Illinois in 1980. She is a member of the American Library Association, active primarily in the Association for Library Service to Children and the American Association of School Libraries. She is the author of several articles, including "Quality and Elementary School Library Media Collections" (*School Library Media Quarterly*, vol. 25, no. 2, 1997) and "Audiovisual Materials and Programming for Children: A Long Tradition" (*Journal of Youth Services in Libraries*, vol. 6, no. 1, 1992). She is coauthor of several books, including *Managing and Analyzing Your Collection: A Practical Guide for Small Libraries and School Media Centers* (second edition of *Collection Analysis for the School Library Media Center: A Practical* Approach, 2002), and *Bibliotherapy with Young People: Librarians and Mental Health Professionals Working Together* (1997). She is currently working on a textbook for young adult literature.